The British Constitution

Also by Guy Browning

How to be Normal

Never Hit a Jellyfish with a Spade

Never Push when it says Pull

The British Constitution
First Draft

Guy Browning

ATLANTIC BOOKS
LONDON

First published in Great Britain in 2015 by Atlantic Books,
an imprint of Atlantic Books Ltd.

10 9 8 7 6 5 4 3 2 1

A CIP catalogue record for this book is available
from the British Library.

Hardback ISBN: 978 1 78239 803 5
E-book ISBN: 978 1 78239 804 2

Printed in Sweden by ScandBook AB, 2015

Atlantic Books
An Imprint of Atlantic Books Ltd
Ormond House
26–27 Boswell Street
London
WC1N 3JZ

www.atlantic-books.co.uk

This Constitution is dedicated to

The Great British People

(yes, that's you)

ACKNOWLEDGEMENTS

Thanks firstly to my research and development team: Alfred Wessex, Robert Fitzwalter, Wat Tyler, Elizabeth Tudor, James Mill, Edward Coke, William Pitt, William Wilberforce, Daniel O'Connell, Emily Pankhurst and Peter Tatchell.

Thanks secondly to my production and editorial team: Margaret Stead, James Roxburgh, Kate Ballard, Bunmi Western, Francesca Riccardi, Lucy Howkins, Karen Duffy, Ilona Chavasse, Juliet Mushens and Sarah Manning.

Thanks finally to Janet Brown for the superb cover illustration, which manages to be creative, traditional and funny all in one. Much like Britain.

The British Constitution

Why it's time Britain had a written constitution

The British have got along just fine for thousands of years without any kind of written constitution. Exactly eight hundred years ago we had Magna Carta, which established a couple of important points such as the right not to be carted away at midnight and thrown into the Tower of London for no reason.

That seemed to keep us happy for a while. Although, if you look carefully at Magna Carta, you'll see that one of the last clauses is about fish traps in the Thames at Staines. I'm not sure that's equally relevant today. In fact, the world has changed so dramatically in the last eighty years, let alone the last eight hundred, that I think it's time to start again.

What does it mean to be British these days? You can be Scottish, Welsh, English, Cornish; you can originally come from France, Pakistan, Brazil, Montserrat, Romania, Ireland, Tristan da Cunha or Basildon; you can be Christian, Muslim, Jewish, Hindu, Jedi, Atheist or Rosicrucian; you can be black, white, brown, pink and any shade in between; you can be gay, straight, male, female or any shade in between.

It doesn't matter how you're put together, it is how we pull together that's important. And how we pull together is by being British in a lot of quite subtle but actually very important ways.

This British Bill of Rights that I am proposing doesn't have any big, honking headlines such as *the pursuit of happiness* or *the liberation of the workers* or *liberté, égalité, fraternité*. Those all seem to me a little bit excitable and not terribly practical. Instead, it has the ten essentials of being British. It's what makes us different from any other nation, particularly Americans with whom we share our lovely language (sort of).

What makes me qualified to write this? Absolutely nothing. Although the fact that I am not a lawyer is a good starting point. All I am is British of the English variety. But, I'm proud to be British and proud of what makes us British.

I also quite fancied being the man who wrote the British Constitution. It will look impressive on my CV. Besides which, someone had to do it so I thought I might as well have a crack at it to save everyone else the bother. I would also look good on a bank note (on the other side from Her Majesty, obviously).

So here it is. It's our constitution. Enjoy it and let me know if you'd like to amend it in any way.

Best of British to you.

Guy Browning

The British Bill of Rights & Duties

(Or the Essential Elements of being British)

1. Everything should be fair.
2. We will decide what's fair.
3. Form an orderly queue.
4. Don't take things too seriously.
5. Create something wonderful.
6. Respect my stuff.
7. Turn up and muck in.
8. Drink tea, walk dog, talk weather.
9. Don't be a selfish arse.
10. Do your own thing. Let others do theirs.

Established and Promulgated in this the sixty-third year
of the reign of Her Majesty Queen Elizabeth II

I. Everything Should be Fair

Fairness means that everyone has a slice of the cake.[1] In Britain if you help make the cake you can have a bigger slice.[2] But to make sure everyone gets some cake, even a small bit without icing, our government will cut the cake.[3] The trouble with fairness is that there isn't enough of it to go round.[4] People aren't born equal[5] but we should try and give everyone a good chance of making the best of what they've got.[6] If we all make that our aim, then life is more likely to be fair.[7] It's not ideal but it's fair enough.[8]

1. *Not real cake obviously. That's a national obesity crisis you're looking at. By cake we mean the things that make life bearable: somewhere to live, a job, a decent education, that kind of thing.*

2. *Yep still talking about cake. This is rewarding people for effort. The more you put in the more you should get out. Otherwise why bother? We need a nation of cake bakers not just cake eaters.*

3. *Sorry, one more cake thing. We don't want people making one huge cake that they then eat themselves. That's the kind of selfishness and unfairness that rightly causes revolutions. The good thing about government is that it can even things out through taxes. Blimey, I think I just said taxes are good.*

4. *People have always fought over scarce resources. Fairness is a way of sharing without the fighting. But it's a tough battle against greed and selfishness. It's true for individuals and true for society. But come on! Be British.*

5. *Yikes that's a biggie! It's nice to think we're all born equal but we're not. For example I have big ears. Small inequality but sometimes quite noticeable (especially the left one). We all have genetic baggage and we're all born into different circumstances.*

6. *Equality of opportunity!!! Doesn't matter who you are or how big your ears are. The doors are open for you. Same education, same opportunities. That's got to be the British way. Doesn't matter where you've come from, it's where you're going to that matters. Sounding a bit American there I know but we've got to do it our way so what you're born into doesn't determine the rest of your life.*

7. *Like I say it's an aim, a struggle, a direction to plod in. But it's the direction we British have been plodding in for some time.*

8. *Can't say fairer than that.*

Class Rules

i.   Britain has a rigid class system much like India except that our untouchables are at the top. Our current prime minister has overcome the enormous handicap of being posh and upper class to make it to the top political spot.

ii. Britain's class distinctions are so minutely graded that you can slip a couple of classes just by ordering the wrong drink, using an interesting adverb or having one too many zips on your trousers.

iii. The big fault line in the class system is private schools. In order to go to a private school you need an enormous amount of money. Private schools then train you to get the kind of jobs where you make an enormous amount of money.

iv. Oxford and Cambridge Universities used to be a toff production line but no longer. They now have to recruit the brightest however socially murky because universities are increasingly dependent on their commercial spinouts which require real brains.

v.   Our upper classes have inbred (and been taxed) almost to the point of extinction but the ones that survive are now fiercely commercially focused and often quite frightening.

vi.   The British working class is also a threatened species
      principally because most of them have worked too hard
      and inadvertently joined the middle class. We have a
      lower class in this country but no-one belongs to it any
      more. Like third class railway carriages they have been
      painted out as being too depressing.

vii. However we do have a new class called Chavs who are
      generally quite poor and welfare dependent but enjoy
      life enormously which upsets all the other classes.

viii. Multiculturalism and mass immigration to Britain
      have helped break down class barriers as it has made
      the whole game three-dimensional. How do you class a
      Polish barista with a degree in engineering?

ix.   A generation from now the Polish barista's children
      will be British and we can sort the class thing out then.
      Remember, most of our upper class and royal family are
      immigrants.

x.   The two most successful classes Britain are the Lower
      Upper Middle and Upper Lower Middle. Although you
      should never confuse the two.

Rules Pertaining to Money

i. The question, 'How much money do you earn?" is more offensive in Britain than, 'What is your preferred sexual position?' You never ever discuss what you earn, even with your spouse, boss or personal financial advisor.

ii. The British have a very strange attitude to money. We're one of the richest nations on earth yet making a lot of money is seen as a little bit of a betrayal because you've left everybody else behind.

iii. We feel uncomfortable sitting on big piles of cash. It feels much more normal to have debt. Which is why the British people and the government are usually sitting on big piles of it.

iv. We've also never really got over Robin Hood who stole from the rich and gave to the poor. But even Robin Hood never stole more than 50 per cent from the rich which seems to be the highest acceptable limit of taxation in this country.

v. Just to confuse matters we may think making loads of money is a bit naughty but the City of London is the financial capital of the world and no-one knows how to make more money from money than we do.

vi.   Thankfully wealth created by the City is called 'invisible earnings'. As a nation we're more comfortable with the idea that our national wealth is derived from the export of fine cheese and craft beer.

vii.   In Britain it is never acceptable to flash your cash. This implies that you are a banker or a drug dealer or quite possibly both. Because of this we are always the first to use debit cards, Oyster cards, mobile payments – anything other than passing cash hand to hand.

viii.   We're good at making money in this country but we are equally good at giving it away. When it comes to raising money for charity we suddenly lose all our shyness about money and revel in making as much as possible.

ix.   Sadly our charities sometimes become some of the most aggressive money making enterprises whose methods put the City of London to shame.

x.   One of the best things in life is actually free in this country (i.e. healthcare). This wonderful thing sometimes gives us the impression that all the other good things should also be free. Sadly, they're not.

Tax Law

i. Taxes are what you pay to the government whose number one job is to protect you. Taxes are therefore what you pay to stop marauding savages stabbing you to death in your front garden. Put like that taxes don't seem so bad.

ii. VAT is the government's way of taxing you every time you spend the money you have left after taxation. Adding 20 per cent to everything from a car to a handbag sometimes makes you want to take your chances with marauding savages.

iii. The difference between death and taxes is that, while both are inevitable, you can avoid tax. Cash in hand is the main way of avoiding taxes for individuals. Cash in Luxembourg is the main way of avoiding taxes for corporations.

iv. Filling out a self-assessment tax form is like performing an operation on yourself without anaesthetic. It's the closest we get to an honesty test. Many fail.

v. Lots of people seek to avoid paying taxes but are all equally keen on having all their lovely services for free. No tax, no services, big debts. Ask Greece.

vi.   There is a school of thought that we shouldn't pay any tax and that we should just pay for things when we need it. This is a little bit barmy because you try paying for a road just when you need it.

vii.   There is normally a direct relationship between countries where people normally pay their taxes and where corruption is low. In corrupt countries you may get away without paying any tax to the government but you have to pay everyone else to get anything done.

viii. If you choose to live in tax exile you have given up an important part of what is required to be British (i.e. paying your fair share). When the tax rate was 97 per cent it was understandable but not at 40 per cent. That's just being greedy.

ix.   Some taxes are more hated than others. Stamp duty taxes you for moving house probably on the basis that when you're dealing with such a large sum of money you won't notice a couple of grand going to the government.

x.   Corporation tax is paid by businesses in Britain. So your local bookshop will pay business tax but Amazon won't because they claim to be located on a coral reef in the South Pacific or somewhere. Handy but not fair.

Statute of Opportunity

i.   Discrimination is a red light that stops you doing stuff for reasons beyond your control. Opportunity is a green light which allows you to do all sorts of stuff that's actually in your control.

ii.   In Britain we are continually struggling to make sure most people see the green light of opportunity rather than the red light of discrimination. We're still on amber with some things, but we're making progress.

iii.   People don't choose to be discriminated against. That's normally done by other people and you become the victim. Opportunity, on the other hand, involves a very important choice. You have to decide to take advantage of it.

iv.   Some people prefer being a passive victim of discrimination rather than an active beneficiary of opportunity. Sometimes it's easier blaming the system rather than making the system work for you.

v.   When it comes to opportunity, our country goes out of its way not to get in your way. For example it's incredibly easy to set up a business here. In fact the government bends over backward to help you. It's true. Try it.

vi.   The biggest opportunity in Britain is not the pursuit
        of wealth or happiness although you can do both to
        your heart's/wallet's content. The biggest opportunity
        is to change stuff. British society and laws are uniquely
        flexible and respond to determined and passionate
        people.

vii.   Having a good education opens more doors than
        anything else in this country, which is why schools,
        universities and teachers of all types are the guardians
        of the country's future.

viii.   We keep buggering about with education in this
        country but one thing we've always tried to keep in
        mind is that everyone should have a great education
        however poor or disadvantaged they are.

ix.   Whoever you are, doors opened by education lead to
        rooms full of opportunity. It's never too late or early to
        start learning. Opportunity only knocks when you're
        standing by the door fully prepared to go through.

x.   Part of being British is creating opportunities for other
        people. We're a generous people and most of us get as
        much pleasure giving someone else a leg up as we do
        getting our own leg up (if that's anatomically possible).

Guidance Regarding Use of NHS

i.   The first port of call for using the NHS is Dr Google. Simply type in your mild flu-like symptoms and find out how long you have to live. Depress yourself further by clicking on various photos of bodies in advanced stages of disease.

ii.   Making an appointment with your GP is a demanding process which requires you to be at the peak of fitness. To work out when the next doctor's appointment is simply take the number of days Dr Google said you have left to live and add three.

iii.   When you're with the doctor remember they have about two minutes to see you, diagnose you, medicate you and refer you. Any small talk more elaborate than 'hello' seriously reduces your chances of being cured.

iv.   Our wonderful NHS is famous for being 'free at the point of use'. Remember this 'point of use' is the hospital front door not the car park which charges the equivalent per hour of having your hip done at a private London hospital.

v.   NHS hospitals have some of the most advanced medical equipment in the world. What they don't have is a bed. Probably the first chance you'll get to lie down is when you're being slid into a scanner.

vi.   When you're in a hospital awaiting treatment you'll probably be very aware of health tourists. These are people who flock here from all over the world to treat you.

vii. People who can't wait to see their GPs often go to A&E instead. That's because they know that A&E has to see everyone in four hours including people with difficult to pin down, cold-like symptoms.

viii. A&E is the one place in Britain where the standard first come first served queuing system doesn't work. Instead they have something called Triage (which is like dressage for ill people) where people close to death are seen first however bad that makes you feel.

ix.   There are always people on the ward in smartly coloured uniforms who will chat and generally make you feel better. These are the cleaners.

x.   It is unacceptable for the British to criticise the NHS. It is our national blind spot like guns in America, autobahns in Germany and underarm hair in France. It is permissible to have one bad experience of the NHS which serves only to highlight the excellent world class service normally available.

II. We Will Decide What's Fair

In Britain the government is responsible for making sure things work fairly for the benefit of all of us.[1] We decide who our government is by voting for them every five years.[2] If we don't think they've treated us fairly then we can vote them out.[3] We expect our politicians to represent our interests not their own.[4] We get the politicians we deserve so we should encourage the best by voting for the best.[5] Your vote is your voice.[6] If you don't vote you don't have the right to complain.[7] If you think your politicians are doing a poor job then you should try doing better.[8] Nothing is stopping you.[9] It's your vote, your system and your country.[10]

1. *It may not feel like it but the government is actually our servant. National, city and local government. All serving us. How cool is that! It wasn't so long ago most of us were serfs and definitely the servants of the government.*

2. *It's a bit like* Britain's Got Talent *but for politicians. Your vote counts. So if you want to keep them/lose them make sure you vote.*

3. *If they haven't served us properly we can send them back. Just like a faulty hoover. You can't do that when you're ruled by dictators/generals/priests/communists.*

4. *In other countries people want power to get rich. In this country we pay our politicians so they can concentrate on serving us. Remember to let them know exactly what you want them to do for you. They're not mind readers.*

5. *We should pay them properly too otherwise no-one's going to want to be a politician.*

6. *If you don't vote no-one will hear you, no-one will know what you want and you won't make any difference. It's like what they say about the lottery: You've got to be in it to win it. And actually there's a much greater chance of winning at the ballot box.*

7. *A hundred years ago women died to get the vote. Show some respect and vote. (Same struggle for votes for Catholics, Jews, Muslims and the Working Class — all won the hard way so you can vote the easy way.)*

8. *Give our politicians a break. Most of them are doing their best. It's not an easy job especially when you think what kind of boss they have (all of us — yeuchh!).*

9. *Nothing! Why not start a new political party? Exciting colours are still available.*

10. *Own it. Make your ancestors/descendants proud. Bearded revolutionaries may talk about Power to the People but we already have it. We just need to use it.*

The Monarchy

Our monarch may look like an elderly and slightly batty relative but she is in fact the head of state.

The Queen has five functions in the constitution:

   i.   Asking whoever won the election to form a government.
   ii.   Listening to their bonkers plan for the country.
   iii.   Reading out their bonkers plan at the state opening of parliament.
   iv.   Sighing deeply in a small room at the palace.
   v.   Waiting for the next election.

The Queen is head of the Church of the England. In this role she has a number of different jobs:

   i.   Damping down any kind of religious fervour.
   ii.   Reminding the Pope that he's not infallible.
   iii.   Promoting interfaith understanding by regular garden parties.
   iv.   Greeting well-wishers at Sandringham at Christmas.
   v.   High-fiving passing bishops.

The Queen is also the Patron of Many Different Academic, Charitable and Educational Bodies:

   i.   The Royal National Society/Institution/Association for Lifeboats/Birds/Animals/Blind/Automobiles/Architecture/Snowboarding.
   ii.   The Crown & Anchor.
   iii.   The Mint Imperial.

The day job of all paid members of the Royal Family has five KPIs (key performance indicators):

i. Well-wishers greeted.
ii. Posies taken from small children.
iii. Glorious/joyous/solemn weddings/births/funerals provided.
iv. Hours of waving per day.
v. Displays of raw power avoided.

The Queen sits up late in the palace studying to be impartial. She is equally gracious to the following groups:

i. Scots/Welsh/English/Northern Irish.
ii. Commonwealth Countries.
iii. Rejected members of the Commonwealth (the US).
iv. Muslims/Christians/Jews/Hindus/Dawks.*
v. Joyless secularist Marxist republicans.

Fanatical followers of the fundamentalist preacher Richard Dawkins.

By sitting on the throne the Queen provides the vital constitutional function of preventing other types of unsuitable continental style people being President/ Head of State/Emperor

i. Shady ex-industrialists associated with chemical spills.
ii. Trades Union Leaders closely allied to Moscow.
iii. Slightly shell-shocked Generals in bunkers.
iv. Bearded zealots prone to sexual incontinence.
v. Zumba teachers.

It is allowable for younger children of the monarch to be any one of the above but they must pack it in if they ascend to the throne for some reason.

The Rules of Parliament

i.   The parliamentary system is rather old fashioned, wilfully eccentric, slightly bizarre and surprisingly passionate and is therefore completely representative of the British.

ii. The House of Commons is where our elected represent-atives meet. There are approximately 400 seats for 680 MPs. This keeps meetings short and reminds Parliament of the general lack of accommodation in the country.

iii. In action the House of Commons makes an enormous amount of noise and there is a lot of shouting. That is what free speech sounds like.

iv. At Parliamentary Question Time the Prime Minister will be asked difficult and probing questions by the Leader of the Opposition. The traditional answer to the question is another question, a deflection, a repetition or a low mooing sound.

v.   Parliament, like much of Britain, is a semi-detached house. The House of Lords is the most bizarre and an-achronistic part of Parliament and obviously works best.

vi. The Lords acts as a pause button and prevents the House of Commons rushing through ill-conceived legislation. Everyone should have a little House of Lords at home to prevent hasty decisions you later regret.

vii. The real work of government is undertaken in Select Committees where politicians of all parties who know something about a subject sit down and try to make good laws. These are like Super Parish Councils, quite dull but generally well meaning.

viii. Politicians are held to much higher standards of behaviour than the rest of us. The institution responsible for holding them to these higher standards is the media, famous for its own transparency, integrity and impeccable morality.

ix. MPs should spend half their time in their constituencies replying to letters about drains and the other half in Westminster deciding whether to go to war in the Middle East. These two are not to be confused under any circumstances.

x. To drum up votes candidates must knock on people's doors. This breaks the basic principle that the British person's home is his/her castle and puts politicians in the same respect category as Jehovah's Witnesses.

xi. Modern electioneering will incorporate the most savvy strategies of social media marketing. If in return we could then vote by clicking there would be a revolution, which is why we can't.

Local Government

i.   Next time you're walking the dog and an overhanging twig pings into your face you may wonder who's responsible. You have just strayed into the awesome power of the Parish Council.

ii.   When Britain was part of the Viking Empire a very Scandinavian kind of democracy was introduced where local decisions were made by all the local people who could sit under one tree. Parish Councils are a bit like this but indoors.

iii.   Parish Councils aren't just for little rural villages. Town Councils are actually big Parish Councils. The head of a Town and City Council is called a Mayor. The head of a Village Council can just act like one.

iv.   Elections are held for Parish Councils unless no-one is interested and then passing people are press-ganged (or co-opted).

v.   Parish Councils, like Wedding Fairs, go completely un-noticed by most people until a particular life event happens when they suddenly become incredibly important.

vi.   When you are planning an extension to your house or you have problems with your drains you suddenly realise that you love the Parish Council and that the people on it have always been your very best friends.

vii. Although they are indeed a lovely bunch of people sometimes Parish Councils make the mistake of pretending that they're actually a mini-version of The House of Commons and try to make decisions on hedge trimming along party lines.

viii. Because Parish Councils are unpaid the volunteers for it are largely retired and or people who have had a problem with their drains in the past. Radical young firebrands are unusual on Parish Councils although the heart of Che Guevara often beats underneath the v-neck pullover of independent councillors.

ix. Parish Councils are allowed to raise their own money through their own special tax called the precept. You'll notice it at the bottom of your council tax bill and it's around £8. If it's substantially more than this check carefully that your Parish Council isn't meeting in a Versailles-style building with musical fountains.

x. It's very easy to get involved in local government and help improve your community. All it requires is a lot of time and effort given voluntarily. Which of course filters out 99 per cent of the population and explains how the Vikings took over in the first place.

Voting Regulations

i. If you've ever been to the tip to get rid of some old rubbish you'll have felt the beautiful communal atmosphere which is a strange but potent mix of personal detox and civic duty. Election day feels very similar.

ii. Every adult in Britain has the vote. This is what 'Power to the People' really means. You have the power literally in your hands to change the government of the nation. You don't even need to shout.

iii. Not only do we have a vote in Britain but we also have a secret ballot. No-one will ever know who you voted for so you can't be intimidated by paramilitary thugs or aggressive pollsters with clipboards.

iv. Postal voting is also available for people who might not be able to get to the polling station on polling day. This is a useful reminder for many people of how to post a letter, where the letter box is etc. It's also wide open to fraud.

v. Most people in Britain vote everyday online when we click on something we like. We bank online and we find our partners online so there really is no reason that we can't vote online. Except it's supposed to be a secret ballot and there are no secrets online.

(Stub v. Pencil 1834)

vi. More people would certainly vote if you could do it online but we would then miss the beauty of polling day. That's when neighbours you've never met and many you have all walk to one place for a single purpose.

vii. This is a beautiful thing. Everyone says hello but no-one ever says who they're voting for because somehow that would spoil the magic.

viii. The truly magic moment is when you have your ballot paper and you are standing alone in the voting booth with a thousand years of acquired power vibrating in the stub of your pencil.

ix. This is where you can decide to vote for a person, a party, a movement, a government, an idea or none of the above. In our system you're actually voting for your local representative not for the government. This voting system is called Pass the Parcel.

x. When the voting is finished the counting begins and the results are declared. The winner then says thank you to the electorate and promises to rule in the best interests of everyone. The loser doesn't.

III. Form an Orderly Queue

A queue is a line of people demonstrating the principle of fairness.[1] A waiting list is a queue on paper.[2] In Britain, where there are limited resources, people are dealt with in a civilised first come first served manner.[3] Jumping the queue is the greatest of crimes for the British.[4] Queue jumpers put themselves above other people by buying or barging their way to the front.[5] If you do that you're not being British and you go to the back of the queue.[6] Ideally we wouldn't have to queue but we don't live in an ideal world.[7] We don't mind a queue but reducing waiting times is always a national priority.[8]

1.   In the world rankings, Britain comes first, second and third in sheer queuing ability. Queuing is a great way of British people standing very close together but not having to talk to each other because they're all facing in the same direction. It's also a great opportunity to study the back of other people's heads at leisure.

2.   Being put on hold is a telephone queue. Notice how reassuring it is to know how many people are in front of you (even though they are probably seven of the world's most long-winded people).

3.   This works because people who really want things get there first. People who can't be bothered don't.

4.   Burn our flag all day long by all means, but don't jump a queue unless you want to see the British turn ugly. Jumping a queue shows that you think you are better than the other people in the queue. In Britain we don't have people who are better than us (except her glorious Majesty of course). You may speak better, eat better, drive better, dress better but that doesn't in any way mean you are better. In fact it may actually mean you are worse. It's complicated but just accept the fact that all British are equal and behave accordingly.

5.   That's corruption for you. Believe me, a queue is better than greasing palms every day for life's basics.

6.   Or lots of people go in front of you which amounts to the same thing. Still nasty.

7.   And just for the record Sweden isn't perfect either.

8.   Waiting times for housing, medical operations, buses and furniture delivery can never be too short. It's a political priority because revolutions never happen when waiting times are short. The British don't mind a queue but if we can't see the front of it, then we're not happy.

Laws of Queuing

i.   The queue is established when the first person arrives and places himself or herself within one metre of the desired thing, for example bus stop or Boxing Day Sale Event, and must be facing that thing.

ii. Should the first person be further than one metre from the desired thing then this is taken as *general hanging about in the vicinity of* and does not legally constitute a queue.

iii. Cash machines are legally exempt from the one metre rule where a distance of 1.5 metres can be maintained to respect the PIN of the first queueee and also not to make them feel as though they are about to be mugged.

iv. The second person joining the queue must be within one metre of the first person and also facing in the direction of the desired thing. Persons facing in another direction will be deemed to be establishing a queue for a different thing and have no waiting rights with respect to the first desired thing.

v.   The third person in the queue establishes the direction of the queue. Common Law says that queues for cash machines should extend across the pavement blocking the pedestrian traffic past the cash machine.

(Wait v. Turn 1951)

vi.   When queuing overnight, sleeping bags must be occupied for 95 per cent of the time. A five minute comfort break is allowed where the sleeping bag place can be 'held' by the adjacent occupied bags.

vii. Letting somebody into the queue is only legal where that person is a blood relative, someone in current sexual relations with the queueee or a certified best mate. A maximum of one adult is allowed to be 'let into' the queue with attendant children under fourteen (does not apply to school parties).

viii. Queue jumping is the act of deliberately and knowingly placing oneself further forward in a queue than one's time of arrival allows. **Punishment: Death**.

ix.   The Common Law response to queue jumping allows for three warnings:

   • That's the back of the queue over there.
   • There's a queue here, mate.
   • Oi, you're pushing in.

x.   In the event of the verbal warning failing, the queue is then allowed to seethe with resentment accompanied with barely audible muttering.

Complaining Procedures

i. Three popular British phrases are, 'Mustn't grumble', 'Can't complain' and 'It could be worse'. These three mask our pathetic inability as a nation to complain about anything.

ii. In fact most British people have a silent grumble mode which continually monitors the appalling lack of fairness in the world. However, vocalising this discontent is very rarely done in case it is unfair to the person receiving the complaint.

iii. When the British do finally complain they use another three standard phrases: 'I know it's not your fault', 'I wouldn't normally make a fuss' and 'I'm sorry I've probably done something wrong'.

iv. It's standard British practice to start any complaint on the back foot ready to back down immediately and if necessary take the blame and shoulder the cost.

v. What the British don't do under any circumstances is shout. Shouting is what we do to children, animals and the TV. We assume if we do it to another live adult Briton that we will be stabbed shortly afterwards.

vi. Many other cultures conduct their daily business at a much higher volume and intensity than the British. Mediterranean cultures tend to converse one notch below the operatic. In Britain a slightly raised voice is seen as some kind of convulsion.

vii. The internet has been a godsend for complaining in Britain. When you phone to make a complaint you are then asked if you know that you can complain online. Difficult of course when you're complaining about your broadband being down.

viii. There's one kind of complaint that the British excel at and that's medical complaints. When two Britons meet it's absolutely fine to run through all your medical ailments from vascular to venereal. It's a kind of bodily self-deprecation.

ix. Sadly people can take advantage of our pathetic inability to complain. Insurance companies habitually get away with not paying our most basic claims. In America they would be sued. In Britain we just apologise and pay an extra premium for wasting their time.

x. One area where we are good at making our views known is social media. There we can complain about all sorts of things because it only takes a click, you won't be put on hold and you don't have to raise your voice. Nothing will change obviously but at least you've had a quiet grumble.

Sports Rules and Regulations

i.   In sport Britain invented the concept of 'fair play'. Other countries might suggest that's what we do instead of winning. In return, we might say to them that diving and football are actually separate sports.

ii.   When something is clearly unfair in life, British people often use the phrase, 'That's not cricket'. The phrase has become less popular as people realised that they understood how fairness worked but they had no idea how cricket worked.

iii.   Something in our national psyche loves amateurism. We like to think that just the process of someone British pulling on a pair of shorts renders them invincible without any kind of planning let alone training.

iv.   Years of national humiliation across a range of sports, most of which we invented, have taught us the value of professionalism. When competition is global and intense, marginal gains are as important in sport as they are in business.

v.   But we still love the idea of an amateur jockey winning the Grand National or a Non-League side winning the FA Cup or someone turning up and winning the Tour de France on their Raleigh Shopper.

(Bat v. Ball 1794)

vi.   Britain loves sport for the same reason it loves dogs: they get you out of the house, you get some exercise and you meet new people. The difference is with dogs you have to take your poo home in a small bag. This doesn't happen in cricket as far as I'm aware.

vii.   Big sports get a lot of TV attention but more British people are actually out there enjoying other sports like fishing, darts, basketball, bowls, triathlon and rambling. As we speak we're probably inventing new combinations such as dart fishing and ramble ball.

viii.   Another immensely popular British activity is wearing a great deal of expensive sports gear including tracksuits, lycra and body armour and then not moving very far at all from the sofa.

ix.   If there's one thing that excites us more than sport it's sport statistics. Doing sport and exercise is all very well and yes the endorphin rush is great but what really counts is entering your new stats on your spreadsheet.

x.   Extreme sports are popular amongst young people. The basis of these is to find new and exciting ways of killing yourself and then extract the death part. Again, the adrenalin really kicks in after you've finished and you're uploading your GoPro footage to YouTube.

Code of Driving

i. British drivers pride themselves on being among the safest and most courteous in the world. That's because we have mastered almost all of the controls in the car including indicators, brakes, mirrors and steering wheel.

ii. The only thing that stops us being absolutely the best drivers is our willingness to attempt other things while driving such as texting, reading, eating, singing, yoga, and tax returns.

iii. The British sometimes engage in faith driving. For example when merging onto a motorway slip road we drive serenely on in the certain knowledge that the Belgian truck driver has room to pull over, wants to pull over and is not reading Asterix comics.

iv. As you approach a roundabout keep your eyes on traffic circulating from the right until you hear the crunching sound as you hit the car in front of you that's failed to take advantage of the five minute gap to get on the roundabout.

v. Tailgating is the driving equivalent of invading someone else's body space. Tailgaters are like dogs. Speeding up doesn't shake them off but just encourages them to follow you even closer at higher speed.

(Bag v. Belt 1963)

vi.   EU law allows the use of the horn willy-nilly. British law states that the horn can only be sounded on three occasions:

- To denote your arrival outside the house of a person you're picking up on a very cold day when you're in the middle of listening to something rather good on the radio.
- To point out an act of unbelievable stupidity on the part of another road user which requires you to take dramatic evasive action but which nevertheless leaves one hand free for fierce use of the horn.
- Inadvertent tooting with a foot while making love in a Nissan Micra.

vii.   Strict laws also govern the use of flashing headlights:

- To acknowledge your neighbour/friend/partner driving in the other direction, one quick flash is permitted, two where you're not directly behind someone and run the risk of confusing the hell out of them.
- To communicate that another driver is driving like a suicidal lunatic is two flashes of which the second is emphatically prolonged.
- To let somebody in from a side road or other junction, two evenly matched flashes. The correct response by the let-in-ee is one quick flash of their hazards if they can find the button without crashing.

Shopping Laws

i. The British haven't changed much from the Stone Age in that they are still a nation of Hunter Gatherers. The only difference is that this is now called shopping.

ii. Men and women shop in completely different ways. Men need to get something, women need to shop.

iii. Shopping by women comes in two phases. The initial purchase of the item followed normally a week later by the return of the item for a refund so that the process can start again. This allows a continual process of pleasurable shopping without any money ever going to the retailer.

iv. Shopping by men also comes in two phases. The rush purchase of something without trying it on and the rash removal of labels and ditching of receipt. The second phase happens a year later for exactly the same item in exactly the same manner.

v. Charity shops in Britain now sell as wide a range of goods as a supermarket plus some items they'd never sell such as straw shoes from Peru. There are many bargains to be had in charity shops – often the shopping that men have done without trying it on in the past.

vi. Britain is a world leader in internet shopping. This allows us to buy BBQ equipment and sun loungers online and have them delivered to our door without once having to go out in the rain.

vii. On the high street we have a new kind of shop which sells everything for a pound including many items that cost a lot less than a pound elsewhere and packets of things that are a lot bigger elsewhere. The actual money lost at these shops is made up for by the priceless satisfaction of knowing you have a bargain.

viii. A very British trait is to buy something instead of doing something. Many keen gardeners spend more time in Garden Centres than they do in their gardens principally because their own garden doesn't have a tea shop or sell very cheap motoring atlases.

ix. Shopping bags are often more important than the thing inside the bag. When a bag has been obtained from a very expensive/trendy shop this is then used many times for transporting other objects. This is called a Bag for Life.

x. Britain is also a nation of shopkeepers and many people work in shops normally on minimum wage so that the prices in the shops are kept low enough for them to afford when they go shopping.

IV. Don't Take Things Too Seriously

The standard British view is that life is essentially comic.[1] Even when it isn't.[2] Our national sense of humour is like personal central heating that keeps us feeling warm however unpleasant things are outside.[3] Having a laugh about something is how the British bond.[4] It's also the way we keep the arrogant, the know-alls and the shouty extremists in their place.[5] No kind of political or religious extremism can survive ridicule.[6] Laughter itself is democratic.[7] We value things that make us laugh, be they friends, entertainers, businesses or politicians.[8] Best of all, in Britain we laugh at what we have in common, not what makes us different.[9]

1.   *It certainly has all the elements of comedy; bizarre characters, farce, slapstick, confusion, mistakes, disasters, mis-timing, collapsing wardrobes, slobbering dogs, unintended consequences and open manhole covers.*

2.   *Of course life is also full of tragedy. That's when we turn up the blackness of our humour. And what other country could come up with Comic Relief for some of the world's most unpleasant problems?*

3.   *If you can laugh about something you're already more than half way to getting the better of it. Laugh about it with someone else and you're definitely on top of it.*

4.   *We British are not a direct people like the Dutch who say things as they see them. We see exactly the same truths but we think it's rude to point them out. Instead we wrap them up in humour so the truth can be aired with a laugh.*

5.   *We didn't invent satire but we were the first country where you could do it without being invited to drink poison shortly afterwards. The whole country is now pre-satirised and ironic which sometimes makes it difficult to be serious about serious things. But it also means that people who want to be taken very seriously indeed don't get out of the starting gate.*

6.   *Because they're laughable. A good test of whether something is acceptable to British culture is if it can laugh at itself. Fundamentalism and humour just don't mix. Neither can survive the other.*

7.   *No-one can make you laugh (except in North Korea where their leader is always surrounded by laughing Generals who know that if they stop laughing they will be shot).*

8.   *Two words: meerkats and Boris.*

9.   *Don't laugh. It's true. Mostly.*

Banter Clause

i.   Banter is a vital part of British life. It's a way of bonding with someone without ever having to say anything serious about life, love, death, politics or anything else.

ii.   You'll know when someone British likes you when they start being rude to you. They really like you when they start actively taking the mick. They absolutely love you when they build elaborate comedy routines around your worst faults.

iii. Excessive politeness between British people is generally a sign that nobody in the conversation likes each other very much. American-style smiling is also a clue that no-one likes anybody.

iv.   Typically the British have evolved a greeting that it's almost impossible to respond to. The correct response to 'alright' is 'alright'. It's not 'my knee is still giving me problems.'

v.   Similarly 'alright pet', 'alright duck' and 'alright cock' are not inquiries about the wellbeing of your pets, farmyard animals or sexual equipment. They are terms of endearment which are now being banned as part of the ongoing process of removing warmth from British communication.

vi.   The standard and generally acceptable way of greeting someone when you pass them in the street is to totally ignore them as if they were utterly invisible despite the fact that you've been living in the next flat for many years.

vii. When dealing with someone for example in a shop it's absolutely fine to say 'Morning' but adding 'Good' at the front can seem dangerously optimistic.

viii. Full marks are given to anyone who can say something funny. Sharing a laugh with someone is the quickest possible way to bond with a fellow Britain, especially when you're simultaneously experiencing something disappointing, miserable or frustrating.

ix.   Unfortunately the British love of jest means that we're more likely to experience something disappointing, miserable or frustrating because we're too busy having a laugh to complain.

x.   Ending banter is also a fine British art. Once two or more bantettes have been exchanged the exchange must be finished on the biggest laugh. Anything else will seem slightly anti-climactic. Exit on 'you're not wrong', 'mustn't grumble', or 'that's my bus' (even if it isn't).

Unspoken Rules at Work

i.   Avoid meetings. Half of every working day is spent in meetings, half of which are not worth having, and of those that are, half the time is wasted. Just say you can't go because you're in a meeting.

ii.   **Never offer to make coffee** in an open plan office. Everyone waits hours for the first person to say, 'Who wants a coffee?' That person then finds themselves making 4000 cups of coffee and one fruit tea.

iii.   Most emails are biodegradable. If you leave them quietly alone they will eventually become irrelevant. If something really matters, the person who sent it will eventually materialize at your desk.

iv.   Getting ahead means getting noticed by volunteering to do things. Once you get the credit for volunteering, get as far away as possible from the project before the work kicks in. The best way to do that is to volunteer for another project.

v.   Lazy people are remarkably successful in business. When something goes wrong it's generally because someone somewhere has tried to do something. Obviously, if you don't do anything, you can't be blamed when it goes wrong.

vi.   Manage your boss using the power of gratuitous flattery especially relating to their management skills. Always remember that they are as surprised as you are that they're in a management position.

vii.   Answering a phone generally means speaking to a customer or your boss, which will probably result in more work. Only answer the phone if you know it's a social call. Just to be sure, make a lot of pre-emptive social calls.

viii.   The acid test of a management consultant is whether they can say, 'Everything's fine, we'll be off then.' No real consultant can. Instead they will sell you a project that costs just enough to keep your profits suppressed to a level that requires further remedial consultancy.

ix.   Reports are the office equivalent of cones in the road. They are not actually work themselves but they are a big, clear sign that real work might be done at some stage. The easiest way to write a report is to change the names in the last report.

x.   Working from home is absolutely fine. It's also absolutely fine to make yourself at home at work. Between the two it's now possible to completely avoid all meaningful work 24 hours a day.

Laws Pertaining to Extremism

i.   Extremists without exception have some kind of odd arrangement of bodily hair. This will be a beard or a comb-over or sideboards that are a bit too long or a moustache that's a bit too small.

ii. All extremists have unpleasant and abnormal sex lives. That's because sex normally has a lot to do with love and extremists have generally not had enough love in their lives and therefore don't know how to give or make it.

iii. It is impossible to talk to extremists for two reasons. Firstly there's no airtime left because they're talking the entire time, often at great volume. Secondly, extremists don't know how to listen.

iv. Interestingly most extremists don't think for themselves. Instead they have a guru/God/philosopher/icon who does the thinking for them and is handily held to have exactly the same views as the extremist.

v.   Extremists are very passionate and lack all doubt. This makes them very attractive to weak and inadequate people who lack passion and conviction. These then become their followers and generally do their dirty work.

vi. Every extremist has an equal and opposite extremist whose views are supposedly different but whose behaviour is remarkably similar (i.e. intolerant and abusive). All extremists hate the police. That's because the police uphold the law and the law is very clear about the limits of extremism.

vii.   Extremists like to radicalize young people. They do this because they know old people are wise to the dangers and selfishness of extremism. Also older people find marching and manning barricades rather tiring.

viii. Ignorance, poverty and hatred are the compost in which the roots of extremism grow. That's why education, prosperity and compassion are the three most effective weed killers of extremism.

ix.   Freedom of speech allows extremists airtime but at the same time it also allows our free press and social media to highlight, refute and ridicule them. A Twitter campaign, a tabloid headline and vlogger message can bring some very serious pressure to bear on extremists (which is why they're outlawed by extreme countries).

x.   Britain is traditionally very tolerant of people with extreme views and allows them to take advantage of all the British freedoms. However, when extremists threaten to end these very same British freedoms then they rule themselves out of being properly British.

Sense of Humour Rules

i.   Ask foreigners what they think one of the most remarkable British traits is and they will say our sense of humour. Which is odd because no other country claims not to have one.

ii.   Much of British humour is dry. In fact it's so dry that at times it's virtually desiccated. The essence of dryness is to make an amusing or witty remark without giving any hint that you might be joking or that you're enjoying the moment in any way.

iii.   The finest dry remarks go completely unnoticed by everyone except the speaker. This is a major if slightly pointless victory for dryness.

iv.   This kind of British humour is hugely dangerous abroad because they hear us saying one thing when we clearly mean another. To us it's beautifully dry, for the rest of the world it's us being two-faced perfidious hypocrites. Which is funny in itself.

v.   On the other hand bodily functions are also a rich seam of humour for the British. Not that you'd want any bodily functions on your hand!!!!!! With this wetter kind of humour the speaker clearly enjoys themselves when delivering it even if no-one else does.

vi.   James Bond is famous for his throwaway remarks and indeed British people love this kind of witticism so much that they're quite happy to throw away the rest of the conversation if necessary.

vii.   Irony is an unpleasant import. It allows us to say stupid and unpleasant things because 'we don't actually mean it.' If you have to explain you're being ironic then you've only succeeded in being stupid and unpleasant.

viii. Cats do the funniest things. As do dogs. But not in an ironic way, which makes them refreshing subjects for light entertainment.

ix.   The British do panel shows extremely well. That's where you get witty individuals together to talk about the news, trivia, travel or anything really. What this does is recreate the best possible pub conversation with the funniest possible mates you could ever have.

x.   Laughing with people is a wonderful thing and there's nothing better than laughing with people at other people. That's the basis of all the programmes that show other people falling off things, destroying things and generally hurting themselves while being filmed by a so-called friend.

Muddling Through Guidelines

i. On the whole things get done quite well in this country. It's what makes Britain such a good place to live. Our patented British way of achieving stuff is to muddle through.

ii. The British pride themselves on being quietly successful without seeming to make much of an effort and also without having any kind of plan. In fact we look askance at people with big plans who make huge efforts because they often try and invade us.

iii. What makes us successful is having a rough plan and then not worrying too much about how it works out. We are a nation of improvisers. We do things that seem to work despite what the trendy theorists and central planners say.

iv. The British will start something because it seems like a laugh and when things don't quite work out we'll do something a bit different and see if that works.

v. We'll do a few experiments, singe a few beards and we won't lose our sense of humour just because we've failed at something a couple of hundred times. Life is a journey and some stops are just for onward connections.

(Sticking v. Plaster 1816)

vi.   Our way of getting things done is to have a fairly good idea, get people behind you, have a crack at it and improve it as much as you can. If it doesn't work too well, bash it about a bit until it does.

vii.   The British have been muddling through for at least a couple of thousand years now. It's thrown up a few things that you wouldn't invent from scratch but they work surprisingly well – for example our cities, our government, our pubs and our legal system.

viii.   We're a mongrel, dappled, complex, multi-layered kind of country and we look on clean, simplistic, minimalistic solutions with suspicion. We allowed it to happen once in the sixties when we got excited about concrete and lino and flyovers but we're not going to let that happen again in a hurry.

ix.   We're a mashed-up nation with a beautiful textured society that's stronger because it's all interwoven into one great big workable picnic blanket.

x.   It may not be perfect but it's always getting a little bit better and you can be sure that we'll all find a way to muddle through eventually.

V. Create Something Wonderful

Britain is a nation of thinkers and tinkerers.[1] We dream up new sports, new games and new entertainment.[2] We devise great theories of everything from particles to politics.[3] We're good at making things look and feel good in design, fashion and architecture.[4] We also invent fantastic new technologies, machines, medicines.[5] We start new ventures and projects and charities to change the world in small practical steps.[6] Then we add the finance, the law and the beautiful branding to take our ideas to the world.[7] We share and teach and inspire others to think.[8] We're a traditional nation with a gift for creating the future.

1. *In this country you are expected to think for yourself, to have your own opinions. We don't wait to be told what to think. And we don't get punished for thinking whatever we like.*

2. *We're brilliant at formats. That's great ideas for sports and TV programmes which we then export to the world. At sports we used to think it was OK to get beaten because we invented it. Now we invent new ways of winning from the Ashes to the Tour de France.*

3. *Theoretical physicists and scientists are also devising formats but for the natural world. Social scientists invent theories for the way we all behave. Don't forget all these brilliant theories (Marxism, Darwinism, Freudianism, Structuralism, Newtonism, Monetarism, etc.) may not actually work in practice so don't take them too seriously.*

4. *British architects are famous around the world. For being old fashioned? No madam! For being absolutely cutting edge. And then we can build these things because we're once again brilliant at engineering and construction. It's the same at the personal level for fashion and design. Britain oozes creativity from a deep pool of freedom and self-expression.*

5. *We're still the sixth largest economy in the world. And we're just a little itty-bitty island so something pretty amazing must be happening.*

6. *We have a shed/garage/spare room culture, private spaces where we can build oily prototypes, knit radical headgear, knock out hanging beats, stoke the fires of passionate indignation etc. All within arm's reach of a kettle.*

7. *While the world is busy selling us things like washing machines we're busy selling them the banking, law and design that allows them to sell stuff to us. And guess which makes more money? You're right, it's washing machines but a lot of cash comes back the other way.*

8. *Education is one of our biggest exports. People love coming to this country to be educated. We've got great schools and universities and amazing teachers that produce creative free thinkers. Yes, even your teachers.*

Laws Relating to Music

i. The British have a talent for mixing stuff up to produce exciting new stuff. That talent especially applies to music. Give your average young Briton a box full of notes, beats and technology and they will produce a whole new form of music.

ii. Britain does classical music as well as any other country. What we have given to the world is the ability to listen to music while having a picnic outside, in a muddy field under a large umbrella, wrestling with a Scotch egg in the pouring rain.

iii. We have extended this love of muddy fields to rock festivals. These recreate conditions at medieval battle sites but substitute music for arrows. Headlining at Glastonbury is the rock equivalent of conquering Everest except with a lot more tents at base camp.

iv. The British are very good at popular music because of our shed/garage culture and also because British youth are angrier for longer. For the less angry, raves are basically big sheds full of happy people.

v. Rap is very British in that it combines our love of words with our love of music and our indignation about social injustice. Rap is in fact the modern Gilbert and Sullivan with slightly less cross-dressing.

vi.   Stadium concerts are where British people go to get in touch with their pagan past. Rock gods will be on stage, massed lights will be held aloft, there will be a lot of rhythmic swaying and at some stage virgins will be sacrificed.

vii.   A lot of popular music is now manufactured by TV talent shows. Instead of youth rebelling by doing something noisy and unpleasant in a shed, they can vote on TV for their favourite act. And then listen to them on their phone, quietly, upstairs.

viii.   British bands are hugely popular all over the world. Many of these rock bands come from private schools where they may have less to rage about but have fantastic facilities to rage in after prep.

ix   Left alone the British find themselves drawn to music. We have Welsh choirs, gospel choirs, football songs, bath concerts (singing in the bath) and the ever popular singing your head off in the car.

x.   Because the British love and support eccentricity we have also given the world some of the worst music ever. This is especially true with classical music where, because we don't take it very seriously, we don't mind compositions that sound like someone dropping a tray of cutlery.

Entertainment Statutes

i.   If we're honest we British are not very good at being true to ourselves, partly because that might prevent other people being true to themselves. That's why we always jump at the chance of a bit of amateur dramatics where we can be true to somebody else entirely.

ii.   The British love to put on a show because it's an absolutely legitimate excuse to be showy which is normally frowned upon. That's why you'll find your dentist high-kicking in a drag version of *Cabaret*. Perfectly British as long as you change before you go back to work.

iii.   Large charity fundraisers are also popular with us British not just because we're concerned with others less fortunate than ourselves. We prefer to show our concern for others while running a marathon in a tutu, catwoman costume or dressed as a rhino. No other country does this.

iv.   When the British put on a show it's not just for our extroverts. It's also where our technical genius introverts show what they're made of. Village pantos, stadium rock tours, Olympic opening ceremonies and Hollywood special effects are all British techie masterclasses.

(Brucie v. Twanky 1994)

v. Other countries may have more military power than we do but we still have enormous soft power. In terms of global influence Downton Abbey, Harry Potter and Peppa Pig must be worth at least an aircraft carrier.

vi. Britain doesn't make films in the same way that it doesn't make cars. Look carefully and you'll find that a lot of the Japanese cars in Britain are built in Britain and a lot of the American films watched in Britain are also made in Britain.

vii. Where Britain can do it for itself is design. Britain has always been good at marrying art and commerce, which is why our design, fashion, branding, architecture, publishing, media and engineering are so fresh and creative and profitable.

viii Britain does royal pageantry brilliantly although we've now found ourselves in the slightly embarrassing position of having a royal family that's bigger than our army.

ix. To be British you have to walk a fine line between putting on a good show and showing off. That's why cheerleaders have never taken off in Britain.

x. On the other hand if cheerleaders were all dentists high-kicking in drag that would be fine.

The Laws of Science

i.   The British have always been very good at science because it plays to our national strengths: doing odd things in sheds while keeping an open mind and essentially being quite practical about things.

ii. STEM subjects are Science, Technology, Engineering and Maths. Not to be confused with STEM cells which are the little cells from which whole scientists can be grown.

iii. If you ever get seriously ill, there's a very good chance that the drugs you are given will be home grown. Not home grown like herbal tea but the product of multi-million pound research efforts by the world's best scientists in British companies.

iv. British geeks are also some of the geekiest around. Being a geek is now cool and you'll find that lot of the millionaires in their twenties are very geeky indeed. Breakthrough technology needs algorithms that only the geekiest deliver. Respect to British geekdom.

v.   We're also good at concrete. If there's a bridge, a tunnel, a skyscraper or an airport being built anywhere in the world, there's a very good chance that there will someone British in the core team and that tea will be regularly drunk.

vi.   Our Victorian forefathers built much of the modern world but engineering became unfashionable for a while as we experimented with running the world with pan-pipes and a flower in our hair. Now our engineers have rebuilt a lot of things including our global reputation.

vii.   Quantum physics is another dead sexy thing that the British are all over. Ever wondered how computers are going to continue to get faster and cheaper and more powerful? Quantum magic pioneered by lovely British scientists working in university spinouts.

viii.   Cancer? Genetic engineering and genome sequencing are bearing down on it. Again brilliant scientists at the cutting edge often backed by thousands of charity marathon runners at the sweaty edge.

ix.   Britain is one big laboratory. The agricultural revolution started here. So did the Industrial revolution. And quite a bit of the scientific and technological revolutions too. It's because we have the freest of thinkers with the most rigorous of training and finest technical back up.

x.   Science is unlikely to be less important in the future. The best kind of science is done by everyone (man, woman, child) for the benefit of everyone in an open-minded ethically regulated environment. That's us!! Let's have lots more Great British Science.

Advertising and Marketing Rules

i.   Britain is great at having ideas and we're also great
      at selling ideas through advertising and marketing.
      Ridiculously we're very good at selling other people's
      ideas (we have the largest and best advertising agencies
      in the world) but a bit shy about selling our own.

ii.   We're good at thirty-second advertising films because
      we're good at taking the pith. The trouble is we can be
      so funny and entertaining that everyone remembers the
      ad but not the product.

iii. That's better than Euro Advertising. These are ads
      normally for toothpaste that have been made to show in
      every country from Ireland to Israel and feature perfect
      people who don't look quite human.

iv.   There are still a lot of big ads on boards designed to
      capture audiences who are not on a screen (i.e. in a car).
      They assume that people will take their eyes of the road
      long to enough to read the poster. In London, traffic
      goes so slowly you can read the small print.

v.   Poster ads have to be good because Britain has a fine
      tradition of defacing/embellishing posters to deliver
      exactly the opposite message.

vi.   When you have a new product you need a great name.
      Simply take an ordinary word from one area like

music and apply it to a completely different area like cybersecurity. Oboe Security sounds kind of interesting in the same way as the Firewall Orchestra would do in reverse.

vii. But don't get too clever. Trombone Security sounds like you're staffed by circus clowns.

viii. What is spooky with online advertising is once you've looked at one thing once the adverts follow you around the net like a sad dog, even when you've just bought the thing and are unlikely to buy it ever again.

ix. There is no such thing as a free lunch (except in prison bizarrely) and all those things you think you're getting for free on the internet are being paid for by your personal details and preferences being pimped round the net.

x. Of course you can get free things on the net if you illegally download music and films. This is piracy and just means no-one will be able to make music and films in the future. The punishment should be the same as it was for real pirates: a P branded on the forehead. Except hipsters would probably love that.

Rules Relating to Start-Ups

i. Britain has always been a DIY nation. Not just putting up shelves but putting up everything: schools, businesses, buildings, opera houses, railways and far-flung empires.

ii. We then went through a bit of a national wobble when we thought that the State should decide what was best for us rather than trusting people to get on with things themselves.

iii. Thankfully this wobble is now over firstly because we've proved that the State is no better at doing stuff than we are. But, more important, technology has allowed us to do all sorts of things faster and better and more pleasurably than the State could ever imagine.

iv. We're increasingly a nation of entrepreneurs. We have good ideas like we've always had but now instead of giving them away to the American, Japanese or Chinese to take advantage of we build them into businesses ourselves.

v. Our scientists take breakthrough ideas and turn them into world-beating exports. Scientists have always been good at money because that's how they got funding but now they've woken up to the fact that great science is commercial rocket fuel.

(Something v. Nothing 1885)

vi.   Our designers and artists and chefs and musicians are absolutely switched on to earning a living from what they love. What could be a better way of spending your life?

vii.   Creativity is found in equal measure dressed in smart clothing. Our accountants are among the most creative people in Britain. Our bankers are too, although sometimes they get their ethical knickers twisted – but show me an artist who doesn't.

viii.   From British brains come *Harry Potter*, *The Hobbit*, *Winnie the Pooh*, *The Teletubbies*, *Who Wants to Be A Millionaire*, *Coronation Street*, *James Bond*. *Fifty Shades*. All worldwide British export successes. And we do literature too I believe.

ix.   Many of the brains that great new Ideas come from reside in the heads of women. Liberating the female half of Britain to create and build and sell has turbo-charged our creative economy.

x.   Creativity and Innovation are all about fresh new combinations. Britain is really good at social, cultural, linguistic and technological mashups. It's increasingly difficult to be narrow minded in Britain when the benefits of diversity are all around.

VI. Respect My Stuff

Everyone in Britain wants to have the things that make life good for us and for our nearest and dearest.[1] When these things have been earned fairly through hard work we should then be allowed to keep them, enjoy them and pass them on.[2] No-one is allowed to take our stuff without our permission: not an individual, not a business, not the government, not the internet.[3] Property rights give people an interest in society and are the bedrock of freedom.[4] You can't share something if you don't own it.[5] Where no-one owns anything, everyone owns nothing.[6]

1. *House, car, big TV, Xbox, whopping great fridge, strimmer, fluffy towels, sofa, non-stick frying pan, powerful vacuum cleaner, full length mirror, ultra-high speed broadband, hair straighteners and bottles of wine.*

2. *To your children, your partner, your secret lover, the cats' home. Progress in society is driven by people wanting the world to be a better place for their kids. Don't believe me? Have kids.*

3. *So clearly no stealing by sweaty burglars. But no government just helping themselves either (except for lawful but really depressing taxes). And no supposedly friendly social media companies hoovering up our personal data and selling it on without our permission.*

4. *Property rights include you owning yourself. No-one else can own you, trade you or imprison you — that's slavery (and thanks to Magna Carta for reminding King John about that 800 years ago).*

5. *Someone once said that 'property is theft'. I'm not going to tell you who said it because clearly he doesn't think it's important to give people credit for what they've created. When someone creates something you need to give them respect, credit and legal protection. That applies to music, films, design, photos, writing etc. — otherwise it's piracy and theft. Want to make a living doing something creative? Make sure you pay other people for their creativity.*

6. *Sadly, that's the reality of communism. Nice idea, catastrophic outcome. In Britain we let the people do the owning and the State can do a little light redistribution where absolutely necessary.*

Home Rules

i. It's quite difficult to define the modern British home. For the older generation it's where your washing line is. For the younger generation it's where your phone charger is. For the middle generation it's the address your pizza and internet packages are delivered to.

ii. Traditionally an Englishman's home was his castle, especially when he was living in Wales, Ireland or Scotland. This must have spilt over in today's preferred design for a house which is one with a drawbridge (front door), tower (loft conversion) and defensive ramparts (wooden fence) around the house.

iii. In Britain there is one group of people who can afford to buy a house. These are normally people whose parents could afford to buy a house and then benefitted from the 7000 per cent rise in property prices.

iv. The second group of people are those who can afford to rent the kind of houses they'd like to buy. This is called 'generation rent'.

v. The final group are those who can afford neither to buy nor to rent. This group end up in social housing paid for by the state. They will never be on the property ladder because the ladder starts some way above their head.

(Hat v. Hang 1689)

vi.   Quite a few people have second homes. This has the effect of making it more difficult for local people to get their first home.

vii.   A depressingly large number of people have no home at all because they are homeless. Some live rough, some in shelters and some live on the sofas of their friends.

viii.   There are many reasons why most people don't have their own homes but the most basic is that there are too many people and not enough homes. The State has skilfully managed this problem by hugely increasing the number of people whilst failing to increase the number of homes.

ix.   Development of new housing is often stymied by NIMBYs who don't want development in their back yard. The lesson for the future is to have houses so tightly packed that they don't have a back yard. In fact many developers already do this.

x.   The younger generation are waking up to the fact that the best tool for housing lots of people together relatively cheaply is the city. Britain has lots of very liveable cities: Edinburgh, Cardiff, Bristol, Manchester, Southampton, Newcastle etc.

Gardening Bylaws

i.   When you fly into Britain the view reminds you that this is a very green and pleasant land. Things grow here, useful things that you can eat and make stuff with. Or put in a vase to look lovely.

ii.   In our pagan past ancient Britons worshipped nature and worried about climate change much as we do today. They took a very close interest in the sun, the rain, fertility and the seasons. In essence they were, and we still are, a gardening nation.

iii.   British people like to grow stuff. This can be a ten thousand acre estate in the Highlands or a flowerpot in a high rise. Working with nature brings out what's best in our nature.

iv.   Many of the great philosophers and poets have recommended that working in the garden is a great way of bringing inner peace. This may also reflect the fact that great philosophers and poets have probably never been very useful inside the house.

v.   Most Britons aspire to have a garden, their very own piece of British mud. Once you have your garden you can then have a shed in which you can store your summer furniture for 362 days a year.

(Slug v. Pellet 1969)

vi.   Garden centres are like Las Vegas for pensioners. A lot of money is spent gambling that the plant that looks so wonderful on display will one day be equally alive and healthy in your back garden.

vii.   The most popular thing in front gardens up and down Britain is the car. Followed closely by a display of multi-coloured wheelie bins. In the back garden nature reasserts itself with an array of wooden decking from which you can see the rock garden.

viii.   Some British gardens are actually masterpieces of intense and beautifully designed cultivation capturing the sweeping effect of a Capability Brown landscaped estate in a few square feet.

ix.   The reason why Chelsea Flower Show is so popular is that the exhibits are roughly the same size as most people's gardens. It's also useful for people who actually live in Chelsea where the cost of a garden is approximately one hundred thousand pounds a square foot.

x.   For urban dwellers with no gardens of their own, public parks become their communal gardens. The parks they love the most are ones which look like the countryside, not the real industrial countryside obviously, but the city dweller's idea of it.

The Law of Things

i. Because of our weather and because British culture is still basically an indoors culture, we're pretty attached to things. Even though you can't take it with you many people like to collect an enormous number of things they won't be taking with them.

ii. There's an unspoken rule in Britain that the poorer you are the bigger your TV screen is. That's because the narrower your life chances are, the wider you want your window on the outside world to be.

iii. The head of the family holds the remote. Heads of family can often be under ten years old.

iv. Other than our homes, cars are the things we lavish most money on. Hardly anyone drives an old banger anymore because most people now opt for a method of car financing which allows you to always be paying for a car you'll never own.

v. One of the deepest mysteries of the British psyche is our love of delicate porcelain figurines of girls holding doves. Maybe it's because we miss church and are subconsciously re-creating our own uplifting spiritual groves at home. Our maybe people just love figurines of girls holding doves.

(Must v. Have 2002)

vi. Young people are the most attached to things or, to be accurate, thing. Taking a teenager's phone away is like unplugging their life support system. All their vital signs flatline almost immediately.

vii. Bizarrely the most important thing in most British homes is something you can't even see. It's broadband and a home without it is as much use to most people as a house without mains drainage. One of the very rare things it's OK to boast about in Britain is the size of your pipe.

viii. Possibly the most loved thing in the British house is the sofa. All British sofas are bought at massive discount sales with never to be repeated prices. Sofas are now very often recliners which make your traditional non-reclining coach potato look relatively alert.

ix. The kitchen is the heart of every British home and the heart of every British kitchen is the microwave. That little pinging sound is what tells the great British public that it's time to unrecline.

x. All British homes have something in them from somewhere exotic to remind people that they haven't spent their entire life reclined. This often takes the form of a camel or elephant or Buddha or woven straw thing.

Online Behaviour Ordinances

i.   British English is totally unsuitable for communicating online unless there is a special key that highlights sarcasm, irony, dryness and saying the exact opposite of what you mean.

ii.   Whatever you post online ceases to be your property immediately and forever. Nothing truly disappears on the internet apart from your private life.

iii.   The more of your life you spend looking at a screen the flatter your life becomes. Adrenalin rushes, gritty tenacity, rapture, passion, scenes of breathtaking awe and days you'll remember for the rest of your life are not available online.

iv.   It is generally recognised that human interaction is now judged not for what it is but what it might look and sound like online. Your wedding is not consummated until it is on YouTube and your cake hasn't been digested until it is on Twitter.

v.   Selfies are like examining the contents of your own handkerchief – fascinating to you but of very little interest to anyone other than specialist doctors and people who love you very, very much.

vi.   The big internet companies are not your friends. They are selling your private life to other companies you don't know and may not like. Check their terms and conditions. If you're still allowed to.

vii. Yes the government looks at your email. Why not? Everyone else does. The difference is that our government is not trying to sell you something but is trying to prevent you being killed by nutters.

viii. Liking or favouriting or any other one click demonstration of feeling does not constitute engagement or commitment on your part. It demonstrates one click. That's all.

ix.   Lynch mobs now exist on social media. If you believe trial by ordeal and the burning of witches was medieval, don't do the same on Twitter. It's mob rule from your bedroom.

x.   The generation after Generation X,Y and Z will be Generation A. They will start again and know that one real friend who you can have a cup of tea with when you're feeling grumpy and looking rubbish is worth approximately 10,000 online friends and followers.

Body Principles

i.   British bodies don't really have the same reputation as Brazilian bodies but we're nevertheless quite attached to them.

ii. For most of the year British bodies are enswaddled with many layers of clothing which cover a multitude of sins. When we suddenly get our bodies out on holiday it's always surprising how various bits have grown, sagged, inflated, faded and generally become more slug-like.

iii. Obesity is now a national epidemic for which the only cure is huge bags of crisps. It's not really but at the moment that's the approach we're all trying.

iv. The gym is where the British go to work on their body. There are a range of different machines that require you to do movements that would make you look ridiculous without a machine.

v.   Even though people in the gym are virtually naked and sweating heavily, it's one of the least sexy places in Britain. Everyone likes a toned body but no-one looks good on a Nordic skier (unless you're a real Scandinavian, in Scandinavia on real skis).

vi. When the Romans invaded Britain they were greeted by the Ancient Britons who had long hair, died themselves blue and favoured the odd tattoo. Not a lot has changed. Our ancient Britons now dye their hair pretty much any colour of the rainbow including blue.

vii. Tattoos and body art are very popular in Britain and you'd be surprised how many seemingly modest people have a dragon tattoo arising from the cleft in their Royal buttocks. Tattoos are permanent so be very sure of the design and check the spelling. You don't want 'Regret Nohing' on your chest for life.

viii. Piercings are also widely popular from the standard ear piercing to more exotic parts of the face and body. It all counts as body art and we British have a long and colourful tradition of expressing ourselves that way.

ix. We British gave the punk, the Goth and the heavy metal looks to the world. And what did they give us in return? Nothing apart from a lot of good-looking fashionable stuff.

x. Where we draw the line is interfering with other people's bodies without their permission. Female Genital Mutilation is wrong on about sixteen different British levels. Male Genital Mutilation is not much better. God may want a lot of things from us but surely that's not top of his shopping list.

VII. Turn Up and Muck In

Turning up for things is a free choice.[1] Making that choice changes life for you and for others.[2] It's how a free people decides where to focus its passions.[3] It's how friendships, communities and society are made.[4] Mucking in can be done just for fun (leisure), for good (change) or for work (prosperity).[5] We know that if you want something done it's best to do it yourself or with a few friends.[6] That's why we organise ourselves to build, to protest, to celebrate and to improve our communities.[7] The by-product of being involved in something you enjoy, does good and is bigger than you are, is happiness.[8]

1. *You can measure the quality of your life and our society by how many choices are open to you. In Britain we have many choices and it's why a lot of people choose to come here – they value some of the choices we take for granted.*

2. *Ever wonder how some people got where they are today? They quietly made a choice and then turned up. When you turn up things turn out, not always for the better, but mostly.*

3. *Want to build an opera house, a footbridge, a hockey team, a synagogue, a sandwich shop or a model of HMS Victory out of matches? Go ahead. It's your choice.*

4. *All the things we see in Britain today are basically there because at some stage people decided to get up, turn up, meet up and set it up. Schools, businesses, parks, libraries, restaurants, theatres, hospitals, mosques, pet shops, sculptures, clubs, laboratories – all there because someone, somewhere at some time decided to roll up their sleeves and make it happen.*

5. *Motivated teams of people can pretty much achieve anything. Just aim for something good, keep people happy and don't give up. This includes everything from non-league football to eradicating disease although clearly one is more important than the other (you choose).*

6. *Feel like you're powerless in the face of 'the system'? You always have the power to get organised and start doing what you believe in. Don't blame 'the man'. He's just temporarily better organised than you are.*

7. *It's almost impossible to lead a good life in a bad community. Mucking in to improve your community not only does good it also makes you feel good and improves the community which makes everyone feel better.*

8. *Where Americans go wrong is that 'pursuit of happiness' is in their constitution. In Britain we know that happiness is something that sneaks up on you when you're pursuing something else.*

Family Law

i. British society is built on the foundation of the family eunuch (or is that unit – never quite sure). Your family are people you'll always be incredibly close to because you're from the same genetic pool. It might not be a pool you want to swim in but that's the one you've got.

ii. Having a loving family is the best possible start in life because they will always love you however muddy your knees, dubious your taste or disastrous your career. Finding a partner who also loves you like this is the key to the next loving family.

iii. Every family has a member who rejects the family or who is rejected by the family. If you're under fourteen it's probably not your fault but if you're over forty it probably is.

iv. The standard British family is no longer nuclear with a mother and father and 2.4 kids. Instead we have blended families which, like smoothies, can either work very well or can be a really unpleasant combination.

v. Step-parents are not parents that spend a lot of time in the gym. They are parents you acquire because your biological parent failed in one important way (sex, love, money, death). Step-parents have succeeded in this one particular thing but aren't necessarily good at all the others.

vi.   The role of mothers in the family has changed dramatically. They now do all sorts of things outside the house while still doing a lot of things inside the house. But even when they're Chief Executives they're still mum.

vii.   Fathers hold a role of mystical importance in the family. It's mystical because no-one knows quite what it is anymore. Except for kids who know exactly what it is and given the choice would always have a dad.

viii.   Grandparents are an extremely important part of the British family. That's because they now live longer and can babysit grandchildren between the ages of six months and thirty-six years (unless they're on a cruise ship for most of the year).

ix.   Grandparents are also the last group of people in Britain ever to have decent pensions. That's why they live so long and look so happy and can be tapped up for mortgage deposits.

x.   Families, like duvet covers, are exasperating, demanding and emotionally draining. But if you can make one work it's the best thing in the world to have wrapped round you.

Friendship Decrees

i. The average British person has seventy-eight friends in a lifetime. Of those, five are people you've never really liked but were introduced to you by the person you hoped would be your friend.

ii. A friend is someone who accepts you despite all your faults and foibles. Even better they actually find your faults and foibles entertaining and endearing. It's a bit like your family except that friends have actually volunteered to be in your life.

iii. In the same way there is no 'I' in Team, there is no 'end' in Friendship. Sadly, that's not true. In life you slough off friends like a snake sheds its skin. Sometimes you move away, sometime they move away or sometimes they just become a bit of an idiot.

iv. As you get older your oldest friends are the ones you like most. You've known each other so long that history outweighs chemistry. You also don't have to explain anything to them. They know it and they're still around and that's what counts.

v. British people don't make friends very quickly unless they're using the special patented friendship accelerator called alcohol. On the other hand once a British person has decided that you're their friend it's very difficult to shake them off without plastic surgery and a safe house.

vi.   Many people have literally thousands of friends on Facebook or Snapchat. It's perfectly possible to have a very good online friend who you wouldn't ever want to spend time with.

vii.   Social media also makes it possible to get in touch with friends you haven't seen for years and remind yourself why you haven't seen them for years.

viii.   Friends are the people who will listen to all your troubles and then make you laugh about them. They are the ones who will tell you that your new partner is totally unsuitable and a bit of a poop head. They are also the ones that don't get invited to the wedding with 'poop head'.

ix.   You really learn who your friends are when you're too miserable to be social online or off. They're the ones who will come and find you and make sure you're alright – and then not post to the world that you're miserable.

x.   British people will make friends with anyone from any part of the world as long as they don't take themselves too seriously, are willing to have a laugh and make themselves comfortable with continuous and gratuitous British apologising.

Leisure Regulations

i. The British invented leisure time for the masses and we've been making full use of it ever since. In general our leisure activities have divided into what we do outside (sport) and what we do inside (hobbies).

ii. The internet has liberated us from the need to go outside so Britain's number one hobby is now spending time online. Gaming is why you don't see kids hanging around on street corners anymore. Instead they're safely in their rooms playing drug lords vs street pimps.

iii. For slightly older people a great online game is putting all the contents of your garage on eBay. Once you've sold three absolutely useless items, you suddenly decide you're very close to being an antiques dealer.

iv. Other people spend a lot of time searching for absolutely useless items underground with metal detectors. This is like playing the national lottery with digging. There's a good chance you'll win £2 but the chances of getting the pot of gold are a million to one.

v. Sewing and knitting and crafty stuff of all descriptions are incredibly popular in Britain. That's because it's something that occupies your mind and hands and keeps you off the crack pipe.

vi. Sex has also become a bit of a leisure activity for Britons. Online dating, Tindering and Grinding give you all sorts interesting things to do when you've finished your sewing and knitting.

vii. Another basic of life that we've elevated to a national hobby is cooking. Instead of cooking to consume we now spend a lot of time consuming cooking in TV programmes, books and live floor shows.

viii. Britain used to be a nation of collectors with people literally spending a lifetime amassing collections of stamps, coins, beetles and pretty much everything else. Sadly you can now complete any collection with an afternoon's work on the internet so most of the fun has disappeared.

ix. Historical re-enactment is something the British will do at the drop of a Trilby. Societies exist to recreate every age of British history from The Romans to the seventies. Some people can't wait to get out of the current decade so they can start recreating it all in loving detail.

x. The British have a truly bedazzling range of hobbies from naked cycling to moth watching. In fact it's the one thing, dare I say, that we take very seriously indeed.

Community Bylaws

i.   NIMBYs (Not In My Back Yard) are a very powerful group in Britain. Firstly we are a very crowded country and everyone is already in everyone else's back yard.

ii.   Secondly the British are never more active and energetic and passionately alive than when we're trying to prevent change and make life worse for ourselves.

iii.   Nimbys often protest about things that they are in favour of generally but not if it has any consequences for themselves. We're all in favour of new housing, transport, schools etc but not if they create noise or dust or minor vibration during their construction.

iv.   A much more important group is the MATHIMBYs (Making Amazing Things Happen in My Back Yard). These are the positive versions of Nimbys who work tirelessly and often thanklessly to improve their own communities.

v.   The main obstacle to volunteering in the community is the prospect of meeting neighbours you haven't actually met yet even though you've been living next to them for twenty years. The danger is that once you've met a neighbour you can't then unmeet them.

vi.   The British excel at powerful voluntary organizations which get together to raise money for good causes. At the top end we have Unions and Charities and things that start with Royal (lifeboats, birds, animals, children, the blind, Air Force, etc.).

vii. We're also especially gifted at fetes, jumble sales, boot sales, charity auctions, fun runs and sponsored ice bucket/shaving/general personal humiliation challenges. Often these events cost more to put on than they raise but the amount of goodwill and community spirit they generate is immense.

viii. Regular worship is a specialist activity in this country but raising money for church roofs every year is the economic equivalent of Henry VIII's dissolution of the monasteries but in reverse.

ix. For a while the British got out of the habit of doing things for themselves because they were told that the State would do everything. Now that the State can barely afford to blow its own nose, we're rediscovering the power of communities doing it for themselves.

x. Social networking is great for community action especially for communities you can't actually see from where you live. But in the end, just like online internet shopping needs real life delivery vans, community action needs people to go offline and out of their front door.

Regulations Regarding Protest

i.   Throughout British history our peasants have been
     revolting. Ever since we stopped being serfs (thanks
     largely to the Black Death wiping out a large part of
     the labour force) we get a little bit arsy when we think
     things aren't what they should be.

ii. Organised protest is what got us the Magna Carta in
     the first place. We then protested quite strongly when
     our monarchy got too arsy under Charles I and cut
     his head off.

iii. In typical British fashion we thought this might have
     been a bit extreme so we invited his son back to be
     King Charles II. It seemed fair at the time.

iv. We still like protesting. Hundreds of thousands of
     people turned out to protest against the Iraq war and
     even more turned out to protest against the ban on fox
     hunting. Let's be thankful the Iraqis don't hunt foxes.

v.   The British have a proud history of marching against
     oppression which is one of the reasons fascism/
     communism never really took hold here. Many people
     like protesting because it's fun. They just need a placard
     saying Not In My Name.

vi. In the past people have marched against unemployment,
     against evictions and against injustice of all sorts. Today

we tweet and feel as self-righteous as if we'd marched from Jarrow to London.

vii. Online protest comes cheap and easy and can be done with a single click. But it's not quite as fun as linking hands with a thousand other women round a nuclear missile site. In twenty years' time no-one will be reminiscing how they retweeted something.

viii. The British also have a fine tradition of protesting against progress. We love progress as long as it happened some time ago and now has wisteria growing over it. It's now virtually impossible to improve any part of the nation's infrastructure without stirring up clouds of inertia.

ix. Protesters make the mistake of putting themselves in opposition to things. Where protest really works is when you take power and do things the way you want. And then let other people protest.

x. Marches very rarely happen in favour of things which is a shame because that would be a good way of celebrating things. Let's have a free speech day, a free love day, a freedom to worship day, a right to roam day, a national fresh air day, a sexual equality day, a kitemark product quality enjoyment parade. And if we don't get it then we'll protest.

VIII. Drink Tea, Talk Weather, Walk Dog

The British are a naturally reserved people not because we lack passion.[1] We have an emotional queuing system where we wait for others to express themselves.[2] This means that everyone else is waiting for other people to go first.[3] Hence the total silence on public transport.[4] Fortunately the British have three ways of breaking the ice: drinks, weather and pets.[5] Sharing a drink whether hot or cold is the way British people bond indoors.[6] Letting our pets sniff each other is the way we bond outdoors.[7] The totally acceptable ignition for any conversation is the weather.[8] It is always there and always about to change.[9]

1. *The Scots, Welsh and Irish are more in touch with their emotions whereas the English choose to demonstrate theirs through animals.*

2. *The reverse is true online where everyone expresses themselves without knowing or caring whether anyone else is interested or listening. The Victorians used to do the same in diaries or by shutting themselves in a wardrobe and talking to themselves.*

3. *If you wait long enough, the thing you want to express eventually biodegrades to unimportance. This is the advantage of a stiff upper lip. Although for big issues you have to wait ten or twenty years for them to disappear.*

4. *It's not just the emotionally constipated older generation. The young maintain this tradition of silence by always having conversation-killing headphones on. 'Don't talk to me, I've already got someone shouting in my head.'*

5. *Or a cataclysmic national event like a World War or Olympics or World Cup. But normally weather and a cuppa.*

6. *In Britain when it's wet outside we have something wet inside. Tea is physically warming. Alcohol is mentally warming. Drinking anything is great for bonding: it gives you something to do with your hands and your mouth and allows you to demonstrate affection by making or buying the beverage.*

7. *Dogs are basically dating agencies on a lead. Cats do their own dating but without you on the other end of a lead.*

8. *'Cold/Hot enough for you?' is perfect as it uses the weather to make a general inquiry about the other person's comfort levels. It's a miniature queue – let's establish if the weather is OK for you first.*

9. *Where else in the world can you get four seasons in a day and sometimes only two seasons in a year? It's impossible to talk rubbish about British weather because normally it is rubbish.*

Weather Regulations

i. Given that British weather never really amounts to much it's amazing what a worldwide reputation it has. It's a quiet pleasure to see parties of Chinese tourists dressed for a tropical monsoon enjoying some pleasant sunshine in Windsor.

ii. Our weather may be generally benign but our weather forecasting has become increasingly apocalyptic. In the US you will be warned that there is an 85 per cent chance of a tornado moving your house to the next state. Here we use the same tone to suggest that pollen levels are high and if you're going out you might want to take a hankie.

iii. For men who worry about their endowment it's refreshing to see the impact three inches of snow can have.

iv. Scotland can cope with snow and even make money from it. The English are continually taken by surprise by it every year despite snow featuring heavily on just about all Christmas merchandise.

v. To be fair rain does happen in Britain, especially, for some reason, in Manchester. The good news is that it allows us to stay indoors or in the pub or call a cricket match that we're clearly losing a draw.

(Mankini v. Snood 1964)

vi. As a nation of gardeners, no-one really minds rain. What we do object to is miserable drizzle or dreich as the Scots say. Foreigners who come here used to daily heat exhaustion or snow-blindness at home find this weather the most difficult to cope with.

vii. Secretly, this is Britain's favourite weather because it makes us who we are: resilient, stoic, low-key, amused, self-contained and water-proof. We worry about what climate change would do to our national personality. We could become sunny and extrovert and then we might as well be American.

viii. In Britain weather forecasts are usually longer and more complicated than the news. That's because our weather is infinitely complex and of direct relevance to everyone.

ix. In no other country on earth is it impossible to plan for the afternoon's weather let alone for the weekend. Committing to a BBQ in Britain is a slightly smoky version of Russian roulette.

x. The British are absolutely at their finest when at an outdoor event in pouring rain preferably in a foot and a half of mud. These are the ideal conditions for a picnic.

Laws Regulating British Reserve

i. We British aren't reserved. We're actually rather lovely but we don't want to force our loveliness on other people. We like to do a little bit of groundwork rather than rushing in with the 'I love you, man' after five minutes of chit chat.

ii. There's another reason why the British are reserved. It's because the first thing that comes to our mind when we meet people is usually unspeakably rude. We've therefore built in a time delay in order to give ourselves a chance of being slightly more pleasant when conversation gets underway.

iii. In the old days the British restricted their physical contact to a handshake unless you were married to a person and then you could quickly make the leap to full blown sexual intercourse (often with a handshake afterwards).

iv. Nowadays we have intermediate grades of physical contact. We still don't do a lot of social kissing as that's just a French highway to confusion and embarrassment with people biting ears, choking on hair, head-butting, slobbering etc.

v. Hugging is now OK if you're British and we're born after the Falklands War. If you've never heard of the Falklands War you're probably safe to hug. In fact forget about the Falklands War and just hug.

(Wall v. Silence 1944)

vi. In Britain it is generally considered rude to speak to someone unless you've been spoken to. If two people both think like this, conversations just don't get started.

vii. When you've finally spoken to someone British it means a lot. Not quite like mingling blood or seeing each other naked but not far off. A British person then has to say 'Good morning' for the rest of both of your natural lives.

viii. Outpouring of national emotion happens once every twenty odd years in Britain: VE day (1945), World Cup Victory (1966), Death of Diana (1997), London Olympics (2012). For a while everyone speaks to everyone else as if we were Italian and the sun was shining and life was good.

ix. That's so emotionally draining we need twenty years to recover.

x. The British are at their most friendly when they're talking to people who aren't British because we can put aside all our reserve and be the happy chappies we all really are. In fact that's why a lot of us end up living abroad. Although we always keep some reserve in reserve.

Pet Statutes

i.   If you want to know where all the British warmth, passion, communication and affection goes, simply look at our pets.

ii.   In Britain it is perfectly normal for someone to talk more to their pet than they do to any other human being and get everything they need emotionally by doing so.

iii. Pet owners, like child owners, cannot believe that everybody else can't also see how transparently beautiful and abnormally intelligent their cat/dog/horse/goat is.

iv.   The secret to winning the heart of a pet owner is by communicating forcefully and regularly how transparently beautiful and abnormally intelligent their cat/dog/horse/goat is.

v.   What the pet owner hears when you do this is how transparently beautiful and abnormally intelligent they themselves are. Don't take this too far and volunteer to collect their waste in a plastic bag.

vi.   Pet owners take more care over their pet's diet than they do their own. Premium pet food is better for your pet than anything you've ever eaten for yourself ever. Where pet owners sometimes go wrong is then giving their pets seven meals a day.

vii. Dog walkers have an intimate knowledge of their immediate neighbourhood and all the other dogs and neighbours in it. That's how gossip gets passed round neighbourhoods quicker than social media.

viii. Cat owners also have intimate knowledge of all the lampposts in their neighbourhood to which they regularly affix Lost Cat posters. In truth cats are never lost. They've gone to a better world not quite as stingy with food as your one.

ix. In the same way that dogs are man's best friend and cats are woman's best friend and hamsters are children's best friend, reptiles are best friend to people who have no friends and aren't likely to have any in the near future. Not so long as they've got a boa constrictor in their airing cupboard.

x. The British hate animal cruelty and give enormous amounts of money to all sorts of animal charities here and abroad. Many people get a rescue dog that has been abandoned clearly by someone who isn't British. Similarly we don't like seeing elephants made to perform tricks in circuses although we are more than happy to train our dog to do tricks on YouTube.

Laws Regarding Consumption of Alcohol

i. Alcohol is the decompression chamber through which the British like to pass between work and home. This decompression can take place in the pub on the way home or in the kitchen when you get home.

ii. A drink or two acts as an internal Mediterranean climate where things suddenly seem warmer, happier and more relaxed. The hangover the following day is the re-assertion of your internal British climate – grim, miserable and slightly painful.

iii. Binge drinking is a popular British pastime. This is where we get drunk very quickly so that we can shed all our inhibitions and engage in American-style emotional activity with our mates such as random hugging and expressions of undying love.

iv. The pub is one of the great British inventions. The clue is in the name, Public House. It's somewhere where you can feel as relaxed as if you were at home and invite other people to meet you there without having to tidy up first.

v. Pubs used to be places where working men went to get a drink. This has now been replaced by the supermarket where for the price of a hand-pulled pint you can buy enough tinned alcohol to drink yourself purple.

vi. The British like to bond over a drink. Even if you don't drink you should always accept this invitation. Equally powerful bonding work can be done by opening up a packet of crisps on three sides for sharing and then not taking the really big one in the middle of the pile.

vii. There is still a significant section of British manhood whose standard recreational activity is to drink eight pints, punch a bus stop and throw up. This is preparatory work for their later career in government.

viii. A glass of wine with a meal is a civilized tradition that the British have imported from the continent. We've just included breakfast, brunch and afternoon tea in the meals you can have wine with.

ix. Alcohol is extremely influential and many people like to be regularly under it. You should only need alcohol to function if you are a sanitising gel otherwise you're very probably an alcoholic.

x. Violent and abusive drunks often end up in A&E because their behaviour gets a bit medieval. A better destination for them would be the stocks in a public place which is also delightfully medieval.

Rules of the Cuppa

i.   In common law a cup of tea or 'cuppa' can refer to any beverage made with a kettle and hot water. This includes tea made from a tea bag and tea from a pot. All instant coffees are included in the definition 'tea'. You can therefore invite someone round for a nice cup of tea and both have instant coffee.

ii.   Herbal infusions such as peppermint or camomile tea do not legally constitute a 'cuppa' and are strictly defined as a medicine in the enema sub-classification. Earl Grey tea is a legal grey area (much like the tea itself).

iii.   Biscuits form a vital part of having a cuppa. They must always be offered if only for the other person to refuse and demonstrate that they are 'being good'.

iv.   There are strict laws regarding the use of a tea bag. One bag must be used per cup, the bag must be put in the cup before the water and the water must be applied before the milk.

v.   By law the moment when the back is turned to deal with the kettle and pour the hot water is when the vital and impertinent probing question should be asked:

(Cup v. Mug 1896)

- What did the doctor say?
- Sounds like you've had an interesting time.*
- So you're attracted to accountancy.**
- So you've been seeing a lot of Kevin.
- You're looking tired.***

  * *Sounds like a statement but is legally a question.*
  ** *Statements starting with 'so' are an inducement to spill the beans.*
  *** *You're looking ill.*

vi.   When tea is made in a pot the law stipulates a ratio of one bag per person. There are no exceptions to this rule. A beverage prepared with less than one bag per person constitutes coloured water and must not be served to working people.

vii.   Tea bags, like chewing gum, cannot be used more than once except by the criminally insane and insanely tight. Tea bags do not 'regain their flavour overnight' if hung on the washing line.

viii.   Real coffee is coffee where beans are visible, grinding is audible and metal has to be banged aggressively. Do not expect intimate conversation to commence until the grinding and banging is complete.

IX. Don't be a Selfish Arse

Being British means you have all sorts of precious freedoms.[1] One freedom you don't have is the right to hurt other people.[2] You can't physically hurt people[3]; you can't bully or intimidate them;[4] you can't sexually abuse them;[5] you can't steal their property; you can't enslave them or restrain them; you can't lie to them,[6] cheat them or abuse them online or off; you can't spoil or destroy the fabric of our community. Doing any of these means you are not only disgustingly selfish but you are also an arse.[7] You don't deserve to be British and you will be punished.[8] There are no rights without corresponding duties.[9]

1. *These freedoms have to be earned. You're not entitled to them just because you're a wonderful person. You get them because you are signed into the social contract – and that means the law.*

2. *It's unpleasant and it's not the way we do things round here.*

3. *The only legitimate users of physical force in this country are the police, the army and roving sumo wrestlers. It's good that we leave force to them otherwise we all end up carrying guns and no civilized country does that.*

4. *Bullying ruins lives. That's why people do it. But every decent person and country fights against bullies whether they come in the form of one person, one online lynch mob or one extremist movement.*

5. *Sex without consent is assault and rape. No-one consents to be assaulted and raped.*

6. *Lying is an incredibly easy thing to do. Gets you out of all sorts of problems. Except the big one that no-one will ever trust you again. Try doing stuff when no-one trusts you. This applies to people, businesses, charities and politicians. The truth is sacred. Don't abuse it or we'll end up living in a state where lies are the only currency available.*

7. *I thought about other words: pillock, plonker, idiot but they weren't quite strong enough. People who do bad things and hurt other people are not edgy or cool or thrilling. They're not misunderstood or victims or artists. They behave like arses and that's the name for them.*

8. *If you do something bad and break the law then you will be punished. Let's not be shy about it. That's how we keep people on the straight and narrow and protect the innocent.*

9. *There's no such thing as a free lunch (unless you have some kind of voucher). If you want the good stuff from society you have to do your duty. And that means obeying the law, even the little ones that seem quite irritating.*

Criminal Law

i. Blue-collar crime has traditionally been about the redistribution of wealth on a one-to-one basis through theft, robbery and burglary. This is normally followed by white-collar crime when the victim overclaims on their insurance.

ii. White-collar crime is where paperwork is involved. A banker who steals millions through fraud gets about the same number of years in prison as someone who robs a post office. Except the former is unlikely to be caught.

iii. Fraud in the city is so complex that it's very difficult to spot and it only becomes obvious when certain symptoms emerge like the collapse of the entire economy. Most financial crime relies on the fact that some people don't understand the phrase 'if it's too good to be true then it's probably not true or good.'

iv. Bankers and Financial Advisors who defraud and mis-sell pensions and mortgages to the public see what they do as a victimless crime. They just deal with figures and percentages and don't really think that real people will really suffer. It's slow motion theft.

v. The third kind of crime is dog-collar crime where religious leaders commit, condone and cover up abuses by the clergy from child abuse to hate preaching.

vi.   No-collar crime is online crime. This takes as many forms as crime offline. In fact the growth of the internet has been driven very largely by dodgy enterprises such as pornography, drug dealing and gambling.

vii.   When you're not turning up in person to buy goods and services, identity theft becomes a very big opportunity for crime. This is made even easier by the fact that normal people often have multiple sets of identities online. It's like digital fancy dress.

viii.   Hot-under-the-collar crimes are crimes of passion. These are crimes committed in the heat of the moment which often involve violence. Perpetrators often justify their actions as a moment of madness but that moment often involves a lifetime of suffering for the victim.

ix.   Many crimes, of whatever collar, are the result of substance addiction. The three main addictions are alcohol, drugs and money.

x.   Crime is divided into opportunistic crime and professional crime. Both are because people think they can get away with it, maybe just the once or throughout their life. It's normally a rational choice based on how likely it is that your collar will be felt.

Punishment Statutes

i.   When you have a constitution which is basically a set of rules, you also have to decide how you're going to punish people who don't play by the rules.

ii.   Prison works for two reasons. Firstly, it gives everyone else a break from criminals. Secondly, it gives the criminals a break from criminality. Except for the drugs, gangs and violence in prisons obviously.

iii.   In this country we have an odd system where we send people to jail for a certain number of years but then let them out after half the time. Like DFS sofas, prison sentences seem to be permanently discounted.

iv.   Restorative justice is a good idea. This means you have to apologise to the victim of the crime and then do something to make good. This works well if you've knocked over a flowerpot but not so well when you've caused the collapse of the international banking system.

v.   Public punishment used to be popular in Britain with huge crowds turning up for hangings and smaller crowds throwing rotten vegetables at people in stocks. In fact public punishment is still popular except now it's death by tweeting and lynchings by social media.

vi.   Instant violent punishment used to be delivered by a quick flogging. The modern equivalents are parking tickets which are applied and pursued with relentless psychotic tenacity. If only all crimes could be dealt with by privatized parking companies.

vii. Crime is disproportionately committed by drug abusers and the mentally ill. Ideally these people would receive help for their problems before they become other people's problems. Closing our mental hospitals was a crime in itself.

viii. The trade in drugs causes a massive amount of crime, rather than the actual use of drugs. The quickest possible way of removing the crime part is to legalise, licence and regulate its use. And then tax it enough to build mental hospitals for habitual users of drugs.

ix. Shoplifting is a very popular crime in Britain. Some people walk into a shop and then brazenly walk out with whatever they need. Others pay, use the item for a while and then take it back to the shop for their money back. Not exactly shoplifting, more shopborrowing.

x. For some people crime is a lifestyle choice. It's just a lot easier to steal stuff than buy stuff. They've made a rational decision that crime pays. Punishment should be sufficient to make them recalculate that it really doesn't.

The Law Regarding Litter

i. Britain is a small, crowded country. If everyone dropped all their packaging at once we would drown in it within six years. That's why in even smaller and more crowded countries like Singapore, littering is punishable by death (I think).

ii. Dropping litter seems like a very small crime compared to big ones like assassinating the cabinet but it isn't. When you drop litter you are demonstrating that you think your immediate convenience is more important than the wider health of the community. That's why you should be shot to focus your mind.

iii. It is permissible to throw away items that you know to be biodegradable such as apples, bananas and other fruits. Be careful throwing coconuts.

iv. Beer cans are not biodegradable although once you've had a few, you might forget this. Death by firing squad will refresh your memory.

v. Care must be taken even when discarding biodegradable waste. For example it's hugely antisocial to drop your banana skin outside the exit of a hospital specialising in hip replacements.

vi. There is a particular kind of littering which comprises a sandwich box, a can of drink, a packet of crisps and possibly a cigarette packet all in one ugly blotch. This is van rubbish, dropped by drivers having their lunch in places that were once areas of outstanding natural beauty. Punishment: being run over by your own van until you are dead.

vii. Litter is often found within ten metres of a litter bin. This demonstrates that the person dropping the litter is either blind, horribly disabled or disgustingly antisocial. It's normally the latter and that person should be killed by the bite of a cobra within ten metres of the antidote.

viii. Cigarette stubs are litter. People who drop them should be killed by a lingering and unpleasant disease.

ix. Dropping chewing gum on the pavement is the worst kind of all littering. People who do this should be forced to wear shoes made only of chewing gum. If that is impractical then they should be hung, drawn and quartered (as they do in Singapore I believe).

x. Picking up litter is one of the most noble, self-sacrificing and useful things you can do as a 21st century Briton. Make a day of it and take your sandwiches. Please take your litter home with you. If you forget to do this there is a punishment: death.

Laws of Being an Arse

i.   Not turning up for doctors appointments. Don't complain that you can't get an appointment when you don't turn up for the ones you do get. Punishment: the diagnosis of a symptomless but mildly worrying disease.

ii. Acting like an idiot when abroad. Please don't photograph yourself naked in another country's sacred sites. You wouldn't like it if foreign tourists posed naked on the altar of Canterbury cathedral. Punishment: holidays in Blackpool.

iii. Graffiti in public spaces. Everyone likes a Banksy, no-one likes a tagger. Punishment: painting the Forth Bridge.

iv. Cold calling. The British don't like people speaking to them in the first place let alone persistent, uninvited cold callers. Punishment: to be put on hold for eternity while their call is recorded for training purposes.

v.   Tailgating which is having someone on the motorway drive within an inch of your back bumper. Punishment: having a police officer stand an inch behind you all day.

vi. Pretending to be religious to get your kids into a church school. Punishment: time spent in Hell after your death, proving that God does exist and he doesn't like his name being taken in vain.

vii.   Tax avoidance through dodgy schemes. Your country has given you the chance to be successful so you should literally be paying it back. Punishment: having to spend your life in the company of dodgy accountants.

viii. Rudeness to people serving you in shops, restaurants, opticians etc. Paying for a service doesn't entitle you to forget your manners. Punishment: clothes that don't quite fit, food that tastes odd and glasses that give you a headache.

ix.   Being persistently late without apology. Your time isn't more valuable than other people's time. Punishment: the best things in life will consistently happen half an hour before you arrive.

x.   Parking in Disabled Bays when clearly you're not. This shows that you don't mind disable people struggling from the far end of the car park. Punishment: obviously one day of disability yourself.

xi.   Trolling on the internet. Being ugly and vicious and hurtful on the internet while hiding behind anonymity. Punishment: a visit to a Swiss Finishing School, otherwise known as Dignitas.

Laws of Not Being an Arse

i. Don't spend all your time trying to get your own point of view over. Listen to other people's point of view and you never know it might change yours. Real listening requires you to shut your mouth and open your mind.

ii. Don't think that the world owes you a living. It doesn't. It's hard work for everybody. If the universe smiles on you it's your duty to smile on someone else. Everybody needs a break some time.

iii. Life is difficult enough without you making it more difficult. Are your personal victories coming at someone else's expense?* What kind of victory is that?

perfectly acceptable in ping pong and other sports.

iv. Generally it's fair to say that your needs are no greater than anyone else's so take a moment before you insist that yours come first. Yes the squeaky wheel gets the grease but no-one likes a car with a squeaky wheel.

v. Everyone is insecure including you. Everyone has issues including you. The main thing is to struggle very hard to make sure the issues you have don't then become issues for everyone else. That's just allowing issues to spread like germs.

vi. No-one likes being ignored. Talk to people openly. Communication leads to trust and understanding.

Pretty much all bad things happen through mistrust and misunderstanding because people haven't had a chat.

vii. Be reliable. Don't over-promise and under-deliver. Don't keep people waiting. Pay people promptly. Forgive honest mistakes. Live like the person you'd like to be if you weren't the person you currently are due to lack of attention on your part.

viii. It's easy to cheat and lie and rob and steal. Anyone can do it even in an air-conditioned office. Why not choose honesty? It'll make you sleep better and you won't get hideous painful boils all over your body.

ix. You are not a superior being by virtue of your birth, your gender, your ethnicity, your God, your politics, your car, your house, your education, your looks, your money or your job. Neither is anybody else.

x. You are judged in this world (and possibly the next) on whether you have added to the sum of human happiness or reduced it. It really does work out for the best for you and everyone else if you can avoid being a total arse.

X. Do Your Own Thing. Let Others Do Theirs

Generations of Britons have given blood, tears and sweat to establish and protect our freedoms.[1] In our country you are free to live,[2] talk,[3] love,[4] meet up,[5] worship[6] and vote how you choose to. The absolute bedrock of this freedom is that your freedom is not at the expense of anyone else's freedom.[7] This exceptionally fine balance is grounded in the deep-rooted British tolerance of other people and our sense of fairness between everyone.[8] People and groups who put their own rights before everyone else's have failed in this essential element of Britishness.[9] We embrace other people.[10]

1. *Magna Carta, the Bill of Rights, Reform Act, Emancipation Act, Suffragettes, Trade Unions, the Great War, World War 2, Equal Rights Act. Rights don't just exist in the fresh air. They're a conscious hard-won effort by a society to provide a civilized life for all its members.*

2. *No-one can lawfully kidnap or kill you. Thanks Magna Carta!*

3. *Freedom of speech. You can say anything you like as long as you don't lie about people. That's actually a big deal. Check out what China/Russia/Iran think about free speech and what they do to people who speak freely.*

4. *Consenting adults can express love for another human being in whatever way they choose. It's all love. Be careful though, you might have to leave this freedom at the Departure Lounge because other countries don't agree.*

5. *Fancy gathering a hundred of your mates to talk about something? Go ahead and book the venue and congratulations on having so many mates! Your meeting would be illegal in many other countries in case you and your mates were planning to overthrow the government. True, sad and pathetic.*

6. *Britain has always been a pretty relaxed country when it comes to religion. We're essentially pagan with spiritual yearnings. If you want to worship God crack on, but try and be British about it (see page 127).*

7. *Your freedoms don't come at the expense of other people's freedoms. So how do we square that circle? Tolerance.*

8. *This is the most important part of being British and the most important part of the whole Constitution. We should carve it in stone except that wouldn't be very British. Just because it's the most important thing doesn't mean we have to get too serious about it. Come on!*

9. *What makes you think that you and your beliefs are more important than everyone else's? Get over yourself and get back in the queue.*

10. *Not literally obviously. In Britain hugging is still classified as an extreme sport.*

The Law Regarding Free Speech

i.   Free speech is a very British thing which is surprising for a nation that doesn't generally like making much noise in public. But it's true although you're quite free to say the opposite.

ii.   In this country you can stand up in public and call the Prime Minister a complete idiot who doesn't know his ankle from his clavicle. The worst that will happen is that someone will tell you to keep your voice down because they've got a headache.

iii.   In fact the Leader of the Opposition in parliament has a full-time job telling the Prime Minister about all his failings in great detail. Parliament also has special privileges where MPs can say potentially libellous stuff with complete freedom.

iv.   In case parliament abuse any of their privileges we also have a free press. This doesn't mean the free newspapers you get at railway stations. It means that journalists can publish stories they believe to be true no matter how powerful the person involved: MP, Union Leader, Billionaire, Princess, FIFA President etc.

v.   In case journalists abuse their power of free speech by invading people's privacy then we have a judiciary to clamp down on illegal phone hacking and so on.

vi. We also have lots of different news channels that delight in pointing out their competition's misbehaviour which is always fun.

vii. You can say what you like in this country but you can't lie about people and things. That's libel and then the other person is free to sue you in court for lying. And then the media is free to report on the case. So think twice.

viii. Free speech is a precious right but like all rights can be abused. We should remember that we are a tolerant nation and that there is a cost to hate speech.

ix. Really free speech happens between people when they don't think they're being listened to. This happens in coffee mornings, after-work drinks and in the back of the bus; not online of course because someone is always listening and taking notes there – Google, Facebook or GCHQ.

x. Social media means that everyone is now their own publisher. This increases the power of free expression. But only when people attach their name to it. Where people can publish anonymously, you get people saying things they would never say to people's faces. That's not free speech, that's trolling.

Dating Commandments

i. In Britain we are allowed to fall in love with whoever we please. Arranged marriages still happen but they are now done by computer and you have to arrange them yourself.

ii. Online dating is tricky – who you'd like to go out with and what your looks can afford are two entirely different matters.

iii. There are two types of online dating. The first is where you look at someone's picture and decide whether you fancy them. The second is where the computer runs a complicated matching programme and then you look at the picture and decide whether you fancy them.

iv. We British rarely ask for a date directly as this implies you fancy someone. Instead we ask someone for a drink and then we can pretend we're worried they're not getting enough liquid. If you've met someone through speed dating, remember to slow down for the love making.

v. However well things go online at some stage you have to meet the person in question and that's often where things go pear-shaped. Making your date laugh is always a good start. If this happens before you've said anything that may not be a good sign.

vi.   Going to the cinema for a date is very popular as it still involves a screen and you can text people during the date to say how well it and the film are going.

vii.   Never go to see a film starring gorgeous stars. Your partner will be glued to the screen and you'll look rubbish by comparison. That's why foreign films with ugly people doing very little are the best for dates.

viii.   When British people start to get serious about dating they go out for a meal. Never order Spaghetti Bolognese in a restaurant unless your date has specifically requested to be spattered with tomato sauce.

ix.   It's sometimes a good idea to get a friend to call one hour into your date. This will give you an excuse to leave or book the wedding venue depending on how well it's going.

x.   In Britain weddings are almost as popular as divorces and actually relatively cheap. The younger generation, being the children of divorced parents, are much more conservative. They get married later, have children later and get divorced later.

Sexual Regulations

i.   In Britain sex has changed a lot recently. The Victorians outlawed any kind of sex that wasn't done between a married man and a woman, in the dark, wearing nighties buttoned at the neck (woman) and spats (man).

ii.   Fortunately a lot has changed since then (apart from a small specialised group of people who still very much enjoy the whole buttoned nightie/spats thing. And good luck to them).

iii.   Divorce has changed British sex. Firstly, contraception has divorced sex from reproduction so we can now do it just for fun. Secondly, divorce itself separates us from our partners so we can have sex with somebody else who tickles our fancy.

iv.   It's now fine in this country to have sex with somebody of the same sex. As people have always fallen in love with and fancied people of the same sex, this seems like a common sense approach. The British like a common sense approach almost as much as sex itself.

v.   There's still a lot of straight sex happening in this country and we have now mostly thrown off Victorian prudery and gone back to an earthier more pagan approach (I'm assuming pagans have earthier sex – key selling point I would have thought).

vi.   The back of the bike sheds used to be the main place for early sexual experimentation. Now it is <u>Backofthebikeshed.com</u> and the mobile app that comes with it. Fortunately there are online filters to protect children from smut online. Ask your children how to install them.

vii.   We also have a lot of apps and dating sites that can put you in touch with suitable/unsuitable partners within five metres of you or anywhere in the world. These contacts can lead to hook-ups which sound sexy to anyone who doesn't own a caravan.

viii.   It would be good to say that Britain leads the world in sexual positions but sadly the only one we've given the world is woman on sofa, man in shed.

ix.   The best kind of sex is one within a loving relationship. This doesn't have to be your own loving relationship of course and websites can help you find loving relationships to destroy at will.

x.   The three things that the British are obsessed with and that are covered incessantly by the media are great sex, fine food and the weather. It's reassuring to know that the only one most people experience on a regular basis is the weather.

Culture Laws

i. When you try and define other country's cultures in three words it's pretty easy: wine, cheese, onions. Sausages, lederhosen, motorcars. Hamburgers, guns, films. Saunas, nudity, childcare. Now try it with Britain. Not so easy.

ii. Darts. It's basically an indoor version of throwing the javelin. No other sport has done more to increase the nation's numeracy.

iii. Modern Art. Makes more money with less talent than the City. Surreal.

iv. *Harry Potter*. Single Scottish mum keeps Hollywood afloat for a decade. Awesome.

v. Rolls Royce. Not German cars but British jet engines. Each turbine blade is one of the most advanced pieces of engineering in the world. Reassuring.

vi. Graphene. The most advanced material in the world. Russian scientists, British institution. We need to make sure we keep the brains and the profits in this country. Nasdarovje!!

vii. Wimbledon. Holding our tennis championship on grass because other countries can't grow grass. Brilliant.

viii.   Notting Hill Carnival. Caribbean-style parade on August bank holiday. Almost guaranteed to rain. Beautiful.

ix.   *Les Miserables*. World-beating musical about the French basically being miserable. Uplifting.

x.   Black Cabs. Five years learning the Knowledge when it's all on SatNav. Epic but dangerously quaint.

xi.   Concorde. Still the most beautiful thing ever to take to the air. Apart from Jessica Ennis-Hill in the high jump.

xii.   The SAS. Goes to places, does things and kills baddies other countries just can't reach. One of the many uniformed reasons we sleep easy in our beds at night.

xiii.   Curry. Our national dish brought to us in a thousand Indian restaurants. Except curries aren't Indian and neither are the restaurants (they're Bangladeshi). Another great British mash up.

xiv.   London Olympics Opening Ceremony: the Queen doing a parachute jump with James Bond. Tradition, creativity, humour: that's us, I think.

The Law Regarding Diversity

i. In Britain you can create the kind of person you want to be and, as long as you're not treading on anyone else's toes, then everyone will wish you the best of luck.

ii. Peer pressure is not the reforming power of the House of Lords but something far less useful. It's when teenagers or hipsters or communities force you to be what you're not. It's bullying and not British. Don't put up with it.

iii. If you're gay or bisexual or transgender or lesbian or straight as a plank, the best of British luck to you. Our nation doesn't want to stop you expressing the love you have in your heart.

iv. If you're Pagan or Jewish or Muslim or Hindu or Catholic or Coptic or Lutheran or Rosicrucian or Jedi or None of the Above, the best of British luck to you.

v. If you're black or white or brown or pink or antique saffron or burnt sienna or any other beautiful God-given shade, the best of British luck to you.

vi. If you like Twerking, Waltzing, Morris Dancing, Ceilidh, Rave, Disco, Cha Cha, Salsa, Barchatta, Horah, Flamenco, Bhangra, Polonaise or the Standard Wiggle, the best of British luck to you.

(Patterned v. Plain 2015)

vii.   If you like Fish and Chips or curry or kebabs or Jerk Chicken or Pulled Pork or tagine or borsht or tapas or croissants or satay or pizza or Sweet and Sour or goulash or tofu or pitta, the best of British luck to you.

viii.   If you're a bin man, a lawyer, a postie, a firefighter, an accountant, an athlete, a jeweller, a house husband, a chief executive, an account manager, an engineer, a carer, a shop assistant, a ferry captain, an IT genius, a potato peeler, a sheep shearer or someone currently between jobs, the best of British luck to you.

ix.   If you're a striver, a seeker, a mourner, a lover, a leader, a loner, a supporter, a wanderer, a dreamer, a builder, a teacher, a listener, a dancer, or just a person on the bus to Clapham, the best of British luck to you.

x.   Britain and her Constitution (First Draft) allows you to be who you want to be. It's a deep privilege that has been given to a vanishingly small percentage of human beings in history.

xi.   Be grateful for it, take advantage of it and don't drop litter.

Acceptable British Conversation

Grunting
The weather
Sport
The effect of weather on sport
Pets
The effect of weather on pets
Any kind of self-deprecation
How much other people earn
How lovely the other person looks
How you both slept
What a great night we had
Medical conditions of other people
YouTube sensations
Disdain for politicians
Ghost stories
Other peoples' personal sexual preferences

Your own sexual preferences
Personal spiritual journey
Deeply held political beliefs
Pornography consumption
Personal medical conditions
Borderline alcoholism
Who you might be sleeping with
Unfortunate facial disfigurements
Any kind of self-aggrandisement
How much you earn
Your dog is ugly
And resembles its owner
Unrequited love
Loneliness
Despair
Death

Should you find yourself straying from acceptable to unacceptable conversation simply say one of the following: 'It looks like rain', 'mustn't keep you' or 'where are you actually from?'

Acceptable British Activities

Dodging showers
Rambling
Jumble Sales
Festivals
Zebra Crossings
Fancy Dress
Mixed marriages
Pub Quizzes
Banger Racing
Pantomimes
Charity Fundraisers
Home extensions
'Book' clubs
Allotments
Dog shows
Politeness
Apologising

Barging
Shouting
Mosquitoes
Mass torchlit rallies
Bull fighting
Monsoons
Ice in beards
Kickbacks
Cabbage-based meals
Public portraits of politicians
Distant horizons
Dancing in public
Tub thumping
Tanks on the street
Genocide
Horse steaks

*British people wishing to take part in un-British activities are encouraged
to go abroad and do them. That's what holidays are for.*

How British is your Religion?

Instils unconditional love for your fellow men and women
Accepts that all men and women are one family
Encourages you to improve the lives of others
Brings you inner peace and contentment
Allows tolerance and acceptance of other faiths
Accepts that the mind of God is essentially unknowable
Has leaders who passionately teach all the above
Gives money to desperately needy people
Raises money through bring-and-buy sales
Welcomes all to its place of worship
Respects the rights of women and children
Increases the total amount of peace and love

Decreases the total amount of peace and love
Has no respect for the rights of women and children
Excludes all others from its place of worship
Raises money through fraud and extortion
Gives money to its leaders
Has leaders who passionately teach all the below
Only they know the mind of God
Claim that their way is the only way
Instils hatred and anger in their followers
Requires that you separate yourself from society
Believes that non-believers are sub-human
Encourages the faithful to kill other men and women

If your religion generally falls below the line it will be subject to the standard British generational correction procedure by which your places of worship will empty of young people and eventually be turned into delightfully converted bijou apartments.

Small Rules

Small Rules govern every aspect of life in Britain.
We all instinctively know what they are
but they've never been written down.

I could try writing them all but it would take
me about thirty years. But it's got to be done.

Could you help me out? Pick your area of expertise,
the smaller the better, and then draft The Ten Small Rules.

Here's an example:

The Ten Small Rules of Getting Out Of Bed

1. Have weird dream of dinosaurs mating.
2. Wonder what strange noise is.
3. Hit snooze button on alarm. Repeat.
4. Fling duvet off body.
5. Ignore complaints from other body.
6. Don't get out on wrong side.
7. Step on belt left on floor by idiot.
8. Feel way to bathroom.
9. Resuscitate face. Avoid looking in mirror.
10. Get dressed. Turn trousers right way round.

When we get enough good ones we can turn it into another book. **The British Constitution: Small Rules**

Submit your Small Rules here:

<u>www.thebritishconsitution.uk</u>

(You're right, that address doesn't have a 'co' before the 'uk')

Keep them short, sharp and relatively clean.

Best of British to you.

Thanks. And Sorry.